W9-CYY-775

KEEPING
AMERICA
AT WORK

KEEPING AMERICA AT WORK

Strategies for Employing the New Technologies

Robert T. Lund
Research Professor, Center for Technology and Policy, and Professor
of Manufacturing Engineering, Boston University

John A. Hansen
Assistant Professor of Economics, State University of New York,
Fredonia, New York

68049

JOHN WILEY & SONS

New York   Chichester   Brisbane   Toronto   Singapore

Library of Congress Cataloging in Publication Data:

Lund, Robert T.
  Keeping America at work.

  Bibliography: p.
  Includes index.
  1. Technological innovations—United States.
2. Labor supply—United States—Effect of technological
innovations on.   I. Hansen, John A.   II. Title.
HD45.L86   1985   331.12'0973   85–17900
ISBN 0-471-81563-2

PREFACE

When someone in the prehistoric world first invented the wheel, it is possible that at least one bystander mused, "I wonder how this is going to change my life." Today, with the pace of innovation accelerating and the magnitude of the changes reaching massive proportions, the question of impact is of prime importance to everyone. No longer merely the province of the curious bystander, the assessment of the consequences of new technology has become the arena for serious study by entire organizations.

Impending changes in manufacturing technology are currently at the base of great concern in American society. Pushed by competitive forces and pulled by available new methods, American industrial firms are trying out radically different manufacturing techniques. The potential breadth and scale of these changes are so enormous that the question of how they will affect us, as employees, as customers, or as citizens, becomes urgent. We need to know, because we may have to *do* something to make sure that the full benefit of these changes can be realized and that the negative impact of these changes is moderated.

American industrial enterprise is very much like a gigantic tree. The crown of this tree, with its myriad technological branches, thrusts upward into the future. This crown is supported by a trunk that is the solid reality of present manufacturing capability. Through its roots, which reach deep into

v

the history of industrial progress, the tree is nourished by huge resources of energy, materials, human skills, ideas, insights, accumulated knowledge, and attitudes.

This tree of industrial enterprise stands in an environment of unprecedented technological opportunity. Pervasive, powerful new tools are available to make manufacturing more productive, more responsive, and more beneficial. These same technologies pose serious challenges to all who must plan for, design, select, or work with them, because the way these new tools are used can cause harm as well as good.

The health of American manufacturing has been the object of much concern for nearly two decades. Observers have become increasingly aware that the tree, for all its great size and importance, does not stand alone. It exists in an environment in which there are competing national and international interests. It is being crowded by foreign competitors in its markets, and it must compete with domestic programs, such as national defense, for its resources. There is danger, too, that this tree's root system of past traditions, structures, and relationships may be inadequate to sustain vigorous technological growth and competitive strength. Some of the roots appear to have atrophied; others are pulling strength from the tree. The search for effective strategies, then, becomes (a) a search for those roots which, if encouraged, will produce healthy growth and (b) a search for those roots of past practice or tradition that should be abandoned or cut off.

We can be encouraged by certain healthy roots of American enterprise, even as we share the concerns of others that some traditions are damaging our capabilities and our will to move ahead. Events of the 1940s and 1950s demonstrated the immensely productive power of America's industry, and the great capacity and ingenuity of the American workforce. That era gave us new insights into how people work together, how they are motivated, and how they respond to change. Innovation is another of our traditional strengths. Throughout the past half-century the ability of our scientists, engineers, and production workforce to design and turn out new products and processes has been a vital part of our industrial progress. Industrial innovation has been a product of the high levels of education and training available to many Americans.

Other traditions that lend vigor to our industrial sector are (1) an enormous domestic market for the products of industry, (2) a government that is generally supportive of enterprise, and (3) widely accepted standards for product consistency and quality in most industries. All these factors provide reasons for believing that, given a sense of what needs to be done, America can develop strategies to employ emerging technological opportunities in ways that benefit our society.

Weak and bad roots must be recognized and dealt with. Managerial competence in manufacturing has repeatedly been brought into question in the wake of repeated incursions of foreign products of superior value in our markets. Adversarial relationships between labor and management are a continuing source of friction and waste of human capabilities. Misuse of resources and environment continues to take its toll on progress. These and other encumbrances of a similar nature have not been sufficient to halt advances in industry, but they have served to slow things down. In a world where there are other countries as capable as we to exploit technological innovation, slow response can be lethal. The undernourished or crippled tree will be crowded out by more vigorous growths.

This book has three objectives: (1) to identify and describe those technologies that will have a major impact on the industrial workforce during the coming decade, (2) to define the opportunities and problems that will be encountered, and (3) to suggest strategies by which private firms and public agencies can act to facilitate positive technological change.

The book is the product of a series of studies begun more

than a dozen years ago, culminating in a project sponsored by the Environmental Scanning Association, Inc., a consortium of human resource executives from 16 very large American industrial firms. This group was seeking guidance on how future technology will affect their workforces, and they asked us to study the question. They arranged for us to have access to senior technical and managerial experts in their firms who could assist us in the work.

We are indebted to the many executives of the member firms of the Environmental Scanning Association for their valuable contributions to the project. We cannot identify each of them, because our arrangement is that we will not reveal the sources of our information. Our gratitude for their forthright cooperation, however, is deeply felt.

Special thanks are due to three members of the Environmental Scanning Association, Hal Janssen, Al Prendergast, and Ted Runge, who acted as a steering committee for the study and who provided early support and liaison. We owe thanks, too, to Andrew Martin and James Maxwell of M.I.T., who assisted in providing materials on comparative training policies. The research that underlies the section on retraining programs was funded by the U.S. Congress, Office of Technology Assessment. In the later stages of conversion of our study report into this book, we had the encouragement of John Mahaney, an unusually understanding editor, the constructive advice of two perceptive critics, Alan Kantrow of Harvard Business School and Myron Tribus of M.I.T., and the sensitive counsel of our advocate for clarity of expression, Marilyn Lund. This book is a much better product because of their combined efforts on our behalf. Finally, we wish to acknowledge with gratitude the role of J. Herbert Hollomon, late Director of the Center for Technology and Policy at Boston University, as mentor and motivator for studies such as this.

His recent death is a great loss to all in industry and government who are concerned with technology policy.

While contributions to this study, both intellectual and financial, were made by a large number of individuals and organizations, the opinions expressed here are those of the authors and do not necessarily reflect the views of any of the contributors, except as specifically noted.

We hope our efforts will incite further search for answers to how Americans should prepare for and manage the industrial technology they are able to create. This question may well become one of the critical issues for us all in the coming decades.

Robert T. Lund
John A. Hansen

Boston, Massachusetts
Fredonia, New York
September 1985

CONTENTS

1

INTRODUCTION

On the second floor of an aerospace plant on the west coast a design engineer works with a computer-aided design system to create new part designs for aircraft. In this plant the link between design and production is so immediate that a few minutes after completion of a design the engineer can walk downstairs and see the new part being completed by the production system.

Computer controls installed in a papermaking plant in the Southern United States make it possible literally to "dial up" papermaking machines to make various qualities of paper without shutting down the production equipment. In this plant there are virtually no workers on the production floor. Control of the production process is maintained through computer terminals in a control room that is removed from the production process itself. Workers in the control room can perform experiments and modify the production process even while it is ongoing.

A major U.S. oil company has installed computer controls in one of its refineries. With this single generation change in technology, labor requirements in the plant were reduced by almost 90 percent, while output was maintained at its previous level.

A company that manufactures telecommunications switching devices converted a part of one of its plants into a computer-controlled "flexible manufacturing system." Now it finds that 90 percent of the profit of the plant as a whole is attributable to the flexible system, which takes up only 10 percent of the floor space of the plant.

These are all examples of the effects of new manufacturing technology currently being introduced by a number of companies in the United States and elsewhere. In the coming decades these technologies will become the rule rather than the exception. They will fundamentally change the nature of the work environment for virtually all employees, from factory sweeper to corporate president. They will alter the types of jobs that workers do, the skills that are required, the relationships between labor and management, the way that products are developed and marketed, and even the fundamental structure of firms. Just as we now look back at the development of the moving assembly line as a watershed in the history of manufacturing, so too will we someday look back at this period and conclude that fundamental changes occurred.

When confronted by the prospect of change, a great many people prefer to wait for the change to become immediate and inevitable before taking action. While the forces for transition are gathering, people whose lives may be radically altered will not even attempt to understand the nature of the change or the reasons for it. Even massive changes, if they are slow-moving or evolutionary, may occur with minimum public notice. The agricultural revolution of the 1930 to 1970 period (during which time U.S. agricultural output increased by one-third while the number of people obtaining their incomes from agriculture decreased by two-thirds) was of this kind. It was an enormously important metamorphosis that proceeded slowly, inexorably, and quietly. It directly affected the lives of millions of people and had indirect consequences for the entire population.

Similar changes are now occurring in manufacturing. This book is about truly new production processes that are currently being introduced in selected manufacturing facilities. It describes the new techniques but focuses most closely on the likely implications of those techniques for workers, managers, and consumers. It has not been written for those who are going to wait. It is for those who want to understand, want to prepare for, want to influence, or want to benefit from change.

The perspective is from now to 1995, but the forces that are described and their repercussions will continue to persist for many years, well beyond the turn of the century.

At the heart of the revolution in manufacturing are two basic, pervasive technologies: computer control of production processes and telecommunications-supported information systems. These two technologies, individually and in combination, are producing some of the most dramatic changes ever seen in the industrial world. Their consequences are likely to rank with those of the introduction and use of the electric motor in the late 1800s. As with the electric motor, these new technologies multiply the capabilities of people, extend the use of machines and materials, and alter the basic structure of manufacturing.

To exploit these new technologies for the maximum benefit of our society, answers must be found to three sets of questions. The first set has to do with the way in which the technologies will be used. What are the trends in computer applications in manufacturing processes? How will telecommunications technology be utilized? What will be the effect of applications of these two technologies on current systems of machines and processes? Where will these changes occur? These and similar questions call for a description of the essential nature of future applications of computers and telecommunications in manufacturing, so the character of the changes can be more clearly visualized.

The second set of questions asks about the impacts. What will be the effects of these changes on people working at various levels in manufacturing organizations? What will happen to the nature and organization of work? How will the manufacturing environment be changed? Will the number of jobs change? What influence will these technologies have on the structures of companies and industries? These questions address the human aspects of technological change—who is affected and in what ways.

Changes of this kind are not entirely beneficial. Some people clearly stand to gain and others are likely to be harmed in some way. So the third set of questions relates to the development of technological strategy. What should be done to promote the beneficial effects and alleviate the adverse effects of the technological changes? What can individuals do? How can companies act? What role is there for public institutions and agencies? It is in these areas of impact assessment and policy formulation where organizations must be willing to reassess conventional practices and explore innovative approaches, so actions fit with both the technology and human needs.

The purpose of this book, then, is to provide answers to this series of questions about these two new manufacturing technologies. Subsequent chapters will describe the nature of the technical changes, outline the expected consequences for those working in manufacturing, and identify strategies that will make the most of the benefits promised by these evolving forces in manufacturing. It is written for all those concerned about the future of manufacturing in the United States, regardless of whether they are practitioners, academicians, or public officials, or whether they are laborers, managers, or technicians. All should become involved, because all are stakeholders in a chain of events that will determine, to a large extent, the economic future of this country.

METHODOLOGY

Information about the nature of future manufacturing technology, its expected consequences, and the strategies for dealing with it comes from research studies conducted over a 12-year span at M.I.T. and Boston University. The most recent of these studies, and the immediate cause of this book, was a project begun in 1982 sponsored by Environmental Scanning Association, Inc. This organization is a consortium of major companies committed to improving their strategic planning of human resources through a better understanding of likely future conditions. These firms, whose annual expenditures for R & D in 1982 exceeded two billion dollars, agreed to allow us to interview their technical managers, manufacturing managers, and other executives to gain a perspective on the major changes in process technology likely to occur in the coming decade.

In the course of these interviews we were given access to confidential strategic information about technology implementation plans and about existing installations of advanced manufacturing technology within the firms. We then evaluated this information in terms of the expected impacts of the technology on the firms' workforces.

Because the companies that participated in the study were all members of ESA, our sample was neither random nor was it scientifically selected. Almost all of the firms were very large, recognized leaders in their industries. They represented an enormous spread of products, geographic locations, and technologies.

Nearly half the firms could be considered as leaders in high technology fields—electronics, aerospace, telecommunications, computers, and office automation. Some of the firms were mainly in conventional product fields—basic metals, paper, or oil. Others provided financial or retail services.

The ESA sponsorship, plus our agreement not to disclose proprietary information, opened the doors to senior company officials and their confidential strategic plans. We were permitted to peer into their technological futures and to gain a sense of how these firms plan to adapt to the coming changes in manufacturing.

Because the sample was not selected in a statistically meaningful way, it was not possible to extrapolate from the quantitative results that we obtained during the course of these interviews. We make no claim, for example, to be able to forecast the number of workers who will be displaced or the number of individuals who will be needed in any particular profession in the future. In fact, a principal conclusion of this work is that detailed forecasting of this type is inherently impossible. It will be the decisions made by (a) individual managers, engineers, and other employees of corporations, (b) unions, and (c) public authorities that will shape the future nature and number of jobs in manufacturing. Our intent is to influence the way these decisions are made, by providing a consensus view of future manufacturing technology, by making an appraisal of its probable impacts on the firms, and by suggesting strategies for taking advantage of the opportunities that the future holds.

TECHNOLOGY AS A COMPETITIVE STRATEGY

The producing sector of the United States economy is based on competition. A product must not only be perceived by some fraction of the market as having some utility, but it must have enough perceived value relative to other, similar products so it will be purchased. Manufacturers use a variety of strategies to achieve value in the eyes of their customers. Product innovation, creating uniqueness of function or appearance, is a common approach. Product customization—tailoring each product to an individual user's needs—is an extreme form of this approach. Product quality, an aspect of technological strategy receiving intense attention throughout American industry today, is another course. Higher quality, in terms of appearance and performance, translates in the customer's mind into higher value. It has been shown to command higher prices in the marketplace, even though modern wisdom asserts that high quality need not mean higher cost.[1-3]

Product value is also enhanced by assuring the customer through warranties that the product will be fit for use. Responsive maintenance and repair services reassure the purchaser that a durable product can be kept functioning for an extended length of time. Careful product design and production workmanship are also part of the arsenal of technological alternatives that provide for reliable product performance, ease of servicing, and long product life.

Regardless of the approaches taken to differentiate one's product in the marketplace, the one common denominator in the calculus of value is price. Novelty has a price. Performance has a price. Service has a price. If two competing products have the same price, the product offering the greater value in terms of novelty, features, performance, quality, operating cost, and so on is likely to win. If the products are undifferentiated, like cold rolled steel, plastic resin or nails, the decisive competitive factor in the long run is likely to be price. Wherever there is strong competition, price will tend to reflect the underlying cost of producing and selling the product. A high cost producer is always at risk of having some other firm offer identical or even more attractive products at lower prices. For this reason, even the most innovative firms assiduously work to reduce their product costs. Engineers and managers in all industries are taught to apply learning curve principles to achieve continuing reductions in product cost.[4]

Until the last few decades competition in the American marketplace was largely a domestic affair, with companies vying for customer favor within a fairly homogeneous economy. Costs of labor, materials, energy, and machines were roughly equivalent for all the firms in a given industry. To be sure, the labor rates of auto workers in Detroit were much higher than those of food processing workers in California, and the price of energy in the state of Washington was much lower than that in New York, but within any given product or geographic market, the resource cost differences between competing firms were quite modest.

The massive entry of foreign-made products into our domestic markets has changed the picture dramatically. For more than two decades products that meet or exceed our standards for quality, performance, and style have been entering American markets in increasing quantities. When these products come from countries where wage rates are one-tenth those in the United States, competition takes on an entirely new meaning. Even those U.S. manufacturers who have never exported a single item now face fierce international competition for markets for their products right at home.

Where firms in other countries have cost advantages in labor, energy, or raw materials, the adoption of advanced manufacturing technology by American firms can be an equalizing factor. Companies are using new process technology to make dramatic cuts in production costs. They have been able to introduce unique product features, upgrade quality, and speed deliveries, all factors that contribute to a competitive edge. In recent years there has been increasing emphasis on the development of new processes as a means of keeping American products in the marketplace. New techniques have resulted, and we now have an imposing array of new capabilities using light (lasers, fiber optics), electricity (microelectronics, electron beams, microwaves, plasmas, piezoelectricity), materials (exotic metals and alloys, plastics, composites, ceramics, superconductors) and machines (robots, flexible manufacturing systems, programmable controls, automated testing and inspection apparatus). The list of individual processes that have appeared on the manufacturing scene in recent years is impressive.

The introduction of new process technology has traditionally been used by American manufacturers to produce new products, to mass-produce goods of consistent quality, or to reduce production costs. Now, however, the adoption of new technology assumes a much more urgent character. Stimulated by what Burton Klein calls the "hidden foot" of competition,[5] many companies are now fighting for their existence, having seen their market shares vanish in a few years. Even well-established giant corporations have found they must reorient their strategies if they are to remain profitable.

Finding and using new process technology is not as simple as reaching into the medicine cabinet for a headache remedy. Many firms have learned to their dismay that a purported cure-all can be a killer and that they are now in deeper trouble than they were before, having invested their resources in a process or system that could not be made to work. Any firm that has been in business for more than a few years will have a legacy of experience of failures and near-failures in production systems. This legacy is carried forward in the organization for years in the best of oral tradition: "Remember when we tried to put automatic controls on the coil winder. . . ?" Legacies of failure reinforce the normal human instincts to be wary of the unknown and cause business executives to hesitate before making large financial commitments for process changes. These feelings tend to be echoed throughout the organization, from sweeper to plant superintendent. The consequence is that the corporate decision-maker is torn between the realization that something must be done immediately to respond to competition and the awareness that a precipitous decision to adopt a new technology can lead to disaster.

Technology planning and strategy can be a way out of the dilemma. This is an approach, however, that has not been fully developed. Companies spend enormous amounts on product and market research and put their best talents to work on establishing marketing and product strategy. Similar attention should be given to developing comprehensive plans for the design, development, acquisition, and use of process technology. Technology planning for new processes involves more than the preparation of technical specifications and financial justifications when obtaining new machines or equipment. It must take into account the changes implicit in how the business will function after the change.

In addition to the purely technical assessment of the appropriateness of a technology to accomplish a given task, technology planning should include principles for designing and selecting processes consonant with the needs of people that will work with it. If organizational changes are implied, plans should provide for reorienting organizational relationships or for reassigning personnel. Strategies for introducing the new technology—familiarization and training courses, equipment installation, testing, and debugging plans—must be developed. There must be provision for information support through feedback and control systems. Attention must be paid not only to internal effects, but technological planning should also take into account the impacts on suppliers, customers, and the community as a whole. Then, too, there must be preparation for probable responses by the firm's competitors to the technological initiatives. Finally, for those items of greatest uncertainty or vulnerability, technology planning should develop contingency plans that answer the "what if?" questions.

Technology strategy, then, is the preparation of comprehensive, integrated plans for the way in which an organization will use techniques and/or information. Given the magnitude of the changes inherent in future manufacturing methods, painstaking development of technology strategy will become essential to the success of a manufacturing firm.[6]

Any attempt to consider American industrial policy must be done within a context or setting. The underlying factors that govern the way the industrial system works will determine the feasible policy choices for effecting change. Certain of these factors are so obvious that they are taken for granted. The industrial community is a competitive capitalistic society. Its management is in the hands of professionals who own relatively small shares of the companies they manage. It is bounded and acted upon by a complex legal and regulatory system. It is the direct source of livelihood for 19 percent of the American workforce and an indirect source of income for much of the rest of the economy. It has been the most productive and most innovative industrial system in the world, supported by $44 billion of research and development expenditures annually.[7]

Such factors are basic and generally understood. In the area of manufacturing technology there are also basic factors that must be recognized. These emerged repeatedly during our study, and they will be found throughout the chapters that follow. Because these are not as obvious or well understood, it may be helpful to identify these principal ideas that guide our forecasts and influence our policy options.

It is imperative for American manufacturers that they be able to adopt advanced manufacturing technology as rapidly as possible. It is not simply a matter of producing better, lower cost products for their customers. Survival is the issue. American firms need to learn how to adopt new methods quickly if they are to have a chance of remaining competitive in either domestic or international markets. Other countries not only have advantages in lower labor rates, but many such as Brazil, Korea, and Taiwan are quickly moving into the use of advanced technologies as well. An objective for American manufacturing policy, then, should be to find ways to encourage rapid adoption of new manufacturing processes. A great amount of effort has been expended toward this objective in the development of *new techniques*—machines, methods, processes—but adoption of these capabilities has been slow. The reasons for the slow uptake of the technologies have been largely human and economic, not technical.

People will respond positively or negatively to a proposed change depending on how they perceive they are to be affected by the change. We see negative responses to advanced automation arising as a consequence of perceived adverse effects of the technology on people at all levels in manufacturing organizations. The great economic incentive for technical change, therefore, must be matched by an equivalent incentive to modify the perceived consequences, so change is welcomed.

HISTORIC PERSPECTIVE

Reasons for the expected adverse reactions to new technology are rooted in our industrial history. During the period of widespread mechanization of work that took place in the United States around the turn of the century, new technology was implemented with little regard for its impact on the kinds of jobs that were created or its influence on relationships among workers, managers, and owners. The result was antagonism, suspicion, resistance to change, work stoppages, and occasionally open warfare between labor and management. In short, the manner in which this technology was introduced directly resulted in the combative union/management positions that now hinder the introduction of new technology. If we do the same poor job of introducing technology now that we did around the turn of the century, it may so poison relationships among workers, managers, and owners that successful introduction of new technology will be impossible. Because of the competitive international nature of the markets in which domestic firms now find themselves, the implications of delays in the introduction of new technology are now much more serious than in the past.

When the industrial revolution began to alter the nature of manufacturing in the last century, production processes became subdivided into smaller and simpler tasks, because simpler tasks were more easily learned (and, many would argue, more easily controlled by management). With few exceptions, the individual worker no longer was able to comprehend the entire production process as it converted materials from their raw state into finished products. The tendency was to regard the worker merely as a part of the machine.

There is an interesting possibility that computer/telecommunications technology can bring back the sense of integration and wholeness of the craftsperson into factory work of the future. Rather than further limiting the content of jobs, companies may be able to provide work that entails breadth of information and scope of responsibility far beyond present jobs. Technology makes it possible. Changes in corporate philosophy, however, may be needed to bring it into existence.

FORECASTING OF PROCESS TECHNOLOGY

How can we know what future manufacturing processes will be like? In observing the impact of technology on production processes (as opposed to the impact of technology on the creation of new goods and services) the future is predictable, at least over a time horizon of a decade or so. The implementation of new production processes requires relatively long planning horizons and large capital expenditures. Consequently, this form of technological change is evolutionary, not revolutionary. Examples of recent evolutionary process changes include numerical control of machine tools, continuous casting in steelmaking, and phototypesetting in publishing. Each of these process innovations have been around for 25 years or more, yet each is still regarded as a relatively new phenomenon.

In searching for those technologies that will have primary influence on the manufacturing workforce over the next 10 years, therefore, it is possible to obtain knowledge about them from the engineers and scientists that are presently working with already known advanced techniques and from the manufacturing innovators who have already experimented with these technologies in their firms. It is unlikely that there will be any process surprises of any consequence in the time span of a decade.

THE "TECHNOLOGICAL IMPERATIVE"

It may be because of its evolutionary characteristics that technology tends to be regarded by nontechnologists (and some technologists, as well) as an implacable force with a will of its own. There is a tendency for people to say, "If that's the way the engineers designed it, then that's the way it has to be."

This way of thinking is wrong. A belief of this kind can paralyze any efforts to find more "humane" ways of getting things done. Technology is merely a body of knowledge and a collection of processes that enable human beings to produce what they want. It can be and is guided by social policy that may be driven by any of our basic human motivations: fear, greed, love, need for power, curiosity, compassion, and (all too frequently) by ignorance. Because this is so, technology strategy should be viewed as a means of shaping technology as well as employing it. Fitting technology to human needs is a part of the shaping process.

Engineers and machine designers hold the key to the nature of work in the new automated factories—they design jobs when they design production systems. Yet technical people are rarely trained to appreciate the value of designing machines in such a way that the human jobs associated with them contain meaningful, rewarding work.

It would be highly desirable to have a set of universally recognized principles of design and selection for new technology that incorporates consideration for human needs. Such principles would have to go beyond the mere physical aspects (ergonomics) of human work and would include concepts related to personal involvement, challenge, scope of responsibility, growth, control, social interaction, and so forth. Engineers and designers trained to consider such principles from the outset of new design would have an ingrained sense of which of the technical alternatives available to them are most appropriate for each particular situation.

HUMAN IMPACTS AND TRANSFORMATION STRATEGIES

Because the adoption of new manufacturing technology is so critical to the long-term survival of American industry, our focus is on those strategies that will speed the adoption process. Because we are convinced that the rate of adoption is dependent on human response to the technology and the way in which it is employed, rather than technical limitations, we have concentrated on the human consequences of technological change and on strategies for providing an environment that welcomes change.

For many it has been more interesting to conjecture on prospects for new and improved products—the Gee Whiz! items—made possible by the new technologies and to presume that the existence of opportunity automatically assures that everything will fall into place. These conjectures, however, fail to provide any clues as to effective strategy for accomplishing the needed transformation of American industrial capability and competitiveness. There is little question that new manufacturing technology will make possible marvelous new products. Our concern, however, is that in the absence of a technology strategy that recognizes human needs, these innovative products in our markets will all have labels indicating their origins in other countries.

After briefly describing the nature of forthcoming manufacturing technology in the next two chapters, we then begin the assessment of the likely consequences of the changes. From there we proceed to the development of strategic policy, through a consideration of alternative private and public actions and actors that can facilitate technological change.

2

FUTURE MANUFACTURING TECHNOLOGY

An Overview

The basic processes used to manufacture most products are pretty well established. Many are centuries old. People recognize terms such as weaving, forging, extruding, molding, pulping, plating, grinding, distilling, or milling that are associated with the production of everyday articles of use. There are thousands of such technologies at present. Our search for new technological forms that would modify or displace existing modes of manufacture was something like trying to locate and identify promising seedlings in a mature forest.

Lest we be accused of failing to find the seedlings because of the trees, we can honestly say we found a great many vigorous young growths. On close examination, however, we found that an overwhelming number of new shoots all had the same genetic roots. Those roots came from the computer and its companion technology, telecommunications. The applications varied significantly, but the underlying technical principles fostering change were associated in a great many instances with the computer/telecommunications connection.

By far the most significant technological trends in manufacturing for the next decade or more are:

- ☐ The increased use of computers to control and integrate manufacturing operations and information.
- ☐ The expanding capacity of electronic communication systems to handle enormous quantities of data over long distances at modest cost.
- ☐ The merging of these two technologies to yield a profusion of product and process innovations.

When we examine the range of technical principles and devices that are being applied or are being readied for application, only the combination of computer and telecommunications technologies has the potential for massive technological changes in the coming decade.

If we consider the future as a map, the manufacturing landscape is one dominated by two large rivers of innovations in computer and telecommunications technologies. They are flowing, not independently but toward a common junction, where the power of each is added or even multiplied. Along the banks of these rivers can be seen the applications of these innovations, in much the same way as farmlands can be seen being nourished by irrigating networks. In this landscape some of the other technical principles or devices can be viewed as being independent streams, but many are linked to the two main rivers, either as tributaries or through common connections in the same irrigation system. We may see lasers, for example, as arising from a principle that is independent from either computer or telecommunications technology. Without these two main streams, however, the great capabilities of laser devices might be completely locked up, and they would merely be interesting laboratory devices. As it is, lasers can read, write, and measure at astonishing speeds because of the computers that control them, and they have become a key factor in the exponential growth of telecommunications capacity.

Just as water in a real river has value when it is used, both computer and telecommunications technologies can be seen as *facilitative* means: they make machines, processes, or organizations work smarter, faster, more accurately, more consistently, over greater distances, at less cost and so on. Their greatness depends as much on their multiplicity of applications as it does on their inherent power.

It will be useful to look briefly at the development of these two technologies. They share some common characteristics. Then we can examine what is happening as the two streams merge. Finally, we can consider the other technical principles being applied to manufacturing and evaluate their importance and rates of diffusion.

COMPUTERS

Computers of all kinds—mainframes, minicomputers, microcomputers, microprocessors, and programmable controllers—have invaded every facet of manufacturing. Once the exclusive property of the accounting department or the data processing group, computers are now an established part of manufacturing technology. For progressive firms, the question "Who owns the computer?" has become moot. The answer is: everyone. For most of the factories we visited in this study, dependence on the computer is rapidly becoming universal.

The evolution of computer applications in manufacturing has proceeded in four stages. The first stage was simply an information processing stage, in which computers acted as large, fast, record keepers and data manipulators. Production-related records and plans were put into the computer's memory and were subsequently updated. Periodically, or on demand, the computer would disgorge its contents for people to use. Such information systems gradually became more comprehensive and sophisticated, but in all instances a person or group of persons was needed to translate the information into operating instructions for machines.

In the second stage, in anticipation of the time when computers would be able to control machines directly, they were put to work recording various machine conditions. Flow rates, mixing times, and temperatures were monitored and correlated with product volumes and quality. Broken thread sensors were developed for weaving machines. Tool wear sensors were developed for metalworking machines. In contrast to the first stage, through which almost every firm in every industry has already passed, monitoring technology is still being developed and applied in all industries.

The third stage of evolution in industrial computer applications occurred when individual machines came under direct computer control. This marks the real transition of computers from a passive to an active role in manufacturing. Operating in either open-loop or closed-loop* modes, computers have become an integral part of the process. As the development of inexpensive microprocessors has made distributed computation feasible, computers have not only moved out onto the factory floor, but they have disappeared from view, into the processes themselves. "Smart" sensors, devices that not only sense a given physical condition but also decide what to do with the information, are simple combinations of sensing units and microprocessors. Such devices can communicate with other microprocessors controlling the machine, with central computers controlling systems, and with display panels for human use.

Computer-controlled robots pick up items located for them by computer-controlled vision systems. Computer-controlled punch presses produce metal panels incorporating a wide variety of holes, slots, notches, and cutouts in one pass, changing tools and panel positions in fractions of a second. Computer-automated fabric knives cut out multiple layers of

*Closed-loop control exists when deviations from desired results are fed back to the controlling device in order to correct the deviation. Open-loop controllers are essentially "blind" to deviations and require human intervention.

cloth according to programmed patterns planned by computer.

Computers interact with engineers to assist in product design and to produce fast, accurate drawings. Interactive systems also permit rapid evaluation of alternate production schedules, locate products on the factory floor, summon tools, dispatch orders to production centers, and diagnose machine problems. Other computers control machines that inspect and test components and finished products.

These are only a small sampling of the many applications of computers to machine and process control. Early applications occurred more than two decades ago in the chemical, oil refining, and similar continuous process industries. Now even industries such as textiles, clothing, metal forming, construction materials, and food processing that have been relatively slow in embracing computer-based automation have rapidly been finding uses for the facile, adaptable microprocessor.[8]

While the concept of computer control has been spreading, some industries (or parts of them) have moved to a yet higher level of computer involvement. In this fourth stage the computer or computer network manages an integrated system of processes. Here the computer takes on the transcendent role of integrator or coordinator. Not only does the computer control each of the processes in the system, but it also controls the movement of materials to and from each process, changes tools, inspects the product, adjusts machines when deviations occur, and provides its human bosses with information on how well things are going.

"Computer-integrated manufacturing systems" are now common in chemical processing plants, utilities, refineries, and allied industries in which the process is continuous and essentially unchanging. Such systems appeared in increasing numbers during the 1970s in metalworking industries. Because of the enormous size and economic importance of the metalworking industries (producers of automobiles, commercial transport equipment, industrial machinery, farm equipment, appliances, generating equipment, and many other items), the application of these computer-integrated metal-working systems constitutes a major technological change that should be of particular interest to corporate strategists and policymakers.

Figure 1 illustrates the four stages in the evolution of computer applications in manufacturing and gives examples of specific technologies at each stage.

These evolutionary steps have been facilitated by the increasing capacity and reliability and the decreasing cost of the computer, particularly the microprocessor. From a technical viewpoint, the limitation in the rate of diffusion of computers into manufacturing has often been the lack of precise knowledge about the critical parameters of the process. For centuries, papermaking had been an art, not a science. Until the process variables could be measured and controlled, computers could not be used in closed-loop control of paper machines. Human beings were required to adjust valves, set speeds, change temperatures, and check the results. As better sensors became available and more became known about the process, the computer was brought in, first to monitor and then to control. More recently, computers have taken over the work of coordinating each of the steps in the process, adjusting one stage to accommodate for conditions found in another. The result is a computer-integrated system, in which the "art" of manufacture has been reduced to a complex set of decision rules handled by a distributed computer network and monitored by human operators.

Two computer-based technologies—robotics and flexible manufacturing systems—are central to computer-integrated manufacturing. Robots have gained a great amount of publicity in recent years and there has been much public concern about them, principally in terms of their effect on employ-

I. INFORMATION PROCESSING. Production output, inventories, product quality data, costs, machine performance, standards, maintenance records, etc.

II. MACHINE MONITORING. Process condition sensing (paper web breaks, tool wear, critical temperatures, pressures, speeds, flow rates).

III. CONTROL

Management Information Systems (MIS)	Computer-Aided Design (CAD)	Computer-Aided Manufacture (CAM)
Materials requirements planning (MRP)	Interactive graphics Modeling	Computer numerical control (CNC)
Maintenance diagnostics and planning	Computer-aided engineering	Parts insertion
Production scheduling and dispatching	Parts programming	Parts nesting
Quality assurance		Parts cutting
		Welding
		Robotic control
		Materials storage and retrieval
		Materials transport
		Testing

IV. INTEGRATION

Computer-Integrated Manufacturing Systems (CIMS)
Chemical manufacturing
Oil refining
Papermaking
Flexible manufacturing systems
Automated microchip making

FIGURE 1.
Evolutionary Stages of Computer Applications in Manufacturing

26

ment and the nature of work. Flexible manufacturing systems, on the other hand, have had much less public notice, but are much more representative of the power and the problems that can come from computer applications in manufacturing technology. Both of these forms of computer application are of particular significance to the metalworking industry, but they provide examples of the types of changes occurring in all manufacturing sectors.

ROBOTICS

The industrial robot has received far more public attention than it deserves. Perhaps its anthropomorphic nature arouses more interest than ordinary machinery. Whatever the reason, robots have tended to be identified by the public and in the popular media as the primary technological force in a new industrial revolution. Hundreds of articles have been written about what robots can do, what robots are being designed to do, how the Swedes and Japanese are leading the United States in the exploitation of robots, and what the employment and skills impacts of robots will be. In some of these discussions, robotics has come to mean the entire compass of computer-based automation. Using the term *robotics* in this way tends to cause confusion. The Robot Institute of America defines a robot as:

> . . . a reprogrammable multifunctional manipulator designed to move material, parts, tools, or specialized devices, through variable programmed motions for the performance of a variety of tasks.

This technical definition of a robot emphasizes the two essential features of a robot: *manipulation*, through one or more arms and hands, of workpieces or tools to do work, and *programming* that enables the robot to be readily changed from one task to another. This programmability is normally provided by a mini- or microcomputer. Future capabilities of robots, now being worked on in design laboratories, were listed in a recent report of the Office of Technology Assessment of the U.S. Congress:

☐ Locomotion, some means of moving around in a specified environment.

☐ Perception, the ability to sense (by sight, touch, or some other means) its environment, and to understand it in terms of a task— for example, the ability to recognize an obstruction or find a designated object in an arbitrary location.

☐ Heuristic problem-solving, the ability to plan and direct its actions to achieve higher-order goals.[9]

Programmable industrial robots have been in use now for many years. They have been particularly welcome in situations where the work was hazardous, hot, noisy, cramped, strenuous, or otherwise undesirable. In such jobs the robot's main function is to pick up, move and set down an object, or to carry a tool (such as a paint spray head or a welding head) through a prescribed path according to an established program. In most of these instances the robot stands alone, although its motions must be orchestrated with the activities of other machines in the area. An example of such a robot task is the placing of a metal shape to be formed by forging into a gas furnace, removing the red-hot part, placing it into a forging press, removing the forged part, cooling it in water, and placing the completed workpiece on a conveyor.

With an eye toward the labor-intensive assembly operations in metalworking industries, robot manufacturers have been striving to design robots that are capable of performing assembly tasks. Robots have been designed that can stack components of an assembly; fasten them by screws, nuts and bolts, or welds; and inspect or test the results. In applications of these types the robots tend to operate as individual machines. There may be a battery of robots in a line, however, each with its group of tasks to be performed on the product as it passes on a conveyor belt. Such combinations can now be found in automobile assembly in Japan, Sweden, France, Germany, and the United States.

In most of the applications of robots we have described so far, the effect of placing a robot into a working situation is to remove the equivalent of a worker for each shift the robot works. The one-for-one relationship may not be exact, because added programming, maintenance, and repair is required, and there may have to be some monitoring of the machine's performance. During the initial start-up and adaptation period, these human support tasks may be appreciable, but once programs are written and the robot has been debugged, these requirements become minimal. When multiple shifts and the ability of robots to work in adverse conditions (such as in forging or welding) are taken into account, labor displacement effects appear to be on the order of 2:1 (two workers replaced by each robot), although averages as high as 4:1 are claimed.

Two trends in robotics development are discernible at this time:

☐ A drive toward increasing sophistication in terms of flexibility, capacity, ease of programming, and sensibility (touch, vision, hearing). This trend is being pursued most vigorously by robot manufacturers, research institutes, and universities in the United States.

☐ A movement toward greater simplicity, accuracy, and adaptability within a relatively limited number of degrees of freedom, accompanied by ease of programming and adjustment to alternative tasks. Miniaturization is also found in some models of these robots. This direction of robot design is more typical of Japanese efforts. It is consistent with a desire to incorporate robotic designs into computer-integrated manufacturing systems.

Both trends are directed toward increasing the applications for robots. Sophisticated machines will be needed if robots are to act more like humans in an increasing range of situations. These robots are expensive, however. The installed cost for this type can range from $125,000 to $300,000, depending on the degree of capability required of the robot. Typical of such machines are those made by Cincinnati-Milacron (the T^3 and its successors), General Electric (the P-5 Process Robot or the AW-7 Arc Welding Robot), or by Unimation (models 2000, 4000, or 8000). Machines of this type will have from five to seven axes of rotation, providing a great deal of freedom of movement, and will have load lifting capabilities of from 50 to over 1000 pounds.

On the other hand, simple, reliable, low-cost robots can find many uses in manufacturing systems. Such robots can be made to team up to handle a task. Prices for such robots are in the $6000 to $15,000 range, plus initial setup, programming, and debugging costs that approximately equal purchase costs. At that level of cost, it is feasible to have spare robots in the wings ready to take over for ailing machines. The Seiko (Japan) family of small robots are representative of the simplified approach. These units have load limits that range from 1 1/2 to

9 pounds, have only two or three axes of rotation, but have accuracies that may be two orders of magnitude ($\pm$ .0004" vs. $\pm$ .04") better than the larger, more versatile machines. Although applications of vision-aided, touch-sensitive machines may be more frequently featured in the media, it is likely that the more simple machines will provide the major impetus for robot automation during the coming decade, and they should have the greater effect on human work during this period.

Even though relatively inexpensive robots exist, however, the pace of adoption has been rather slow. Robots are being bought and used by essentially all of the major firms in metal-working industries, but as late as the beginning of 1983 there were only about 7000 robots being used in manufacturing in the United States. These machines are being adopted at what can be described as a normal evolutionary pace, despite the great amount of publicity they have received. The high cost of capital has undoubtedly had an influence on machinery investments, but slow adoption also appears to stem from a lack of widespread appreciation for how to use robots effectively and a lack of trained technical people to design applications. In some instances, the work scheduled to be performed by a robot is found to yield to simpler, less expensive electrome-chanical solutions once attention is drawn to a particular workstation. Or the job may simply disappear, as recently happened in one plant, leaving the robot ensconced in a sophisticated vision-aided testing station, ready to perform a no longer needed job. One firm we visited had ordered a "fleet" of robots. At the time of our visit, fewer than half of the 50 units purchased had a job.[10]

Seven thousand robots cannot have displaced very many of the 4,000,000 people normally employed in metalworking industries. Furthermore, at least part of the displacement that has occurred can be considered desirable—many robots have taken over dangerous or difficult work where humans probably should not be employed. In addition, the firms that are manufacturing, selling, and servicing robots have created new opportunities for work in the metalworking industry. Thus far, the net effect of robot adoption is of minor consequence.

Nor is the pace of usage for stand-alone robots likely to increase explosively in the coming decade. It will probably show a strong growth trend, but the numbers in use by the end of the decade will still reflect the fact that each application must be planned and each robot procurement must go through an engineering appraisal and a financial justification before a commitment is made. Under such circumstances, evolutionary growth is about all that can be expected. One recent forecast estimates that a minimum of 50,000 and a maximum of 100,000 robots will be in use in the United States by 1990.[11] If the rate needed to reach the 50,000 figure by 1990 were extrapolated to 1995, the number of robots in use will have expanded to 200,000. At the higher rate, the number would reach 600,000. The annual growth rate needed to reach this latter number is in excess of 45 percent, almost double the historic rate of growth of the population of computers in industry.[11] It is unlikely that the growth rate of robots as we now know them will exceed that for computers, so the lower estimate appears to be a more reasonable expectation.

On the basis of a two-for-one displacement of people by robots, we might expect to see a gross displacement of about 400,000 workers by 1995. Overall employment effects are likely to be substantially less because of the creation of jobs in robot making, selling, and servicing. These numbers are large enough to be of some concern to people watching trends in industrial employment, but they are not so large that they should generate widespread concern that the coming of robots marks the imminent end of industrial jobs.

FLEXIBLE MANUFACTURING SYSTEMS

Computer-integrated manufacturing systems effectively demonstrate the enormous power of the coalescence of computers, communications, and machine technology. They make extensive use of a computer system's potential for handling massive volumes of data from a number of independent sources and using the data to control simultaneously the functions of many machines. No human or group of humans can perform the coordinating tasks in the small amount of time required by systems of this kind.

Although there are no useful forecasts of displacement consequences from the general application of these systems, computer-integrated manufacturing systems have the potential to be the primary cause of labor displacement over the next two decades, as well as the primary cause of major organizational changes. They effectively illustrate the extent to which the computer can revolutionize manufacturing.

In the parts fabrication and finishing stages of discrete product manufacture in the metalworking industries, a type of computer-integrated manufacturing system is being used with increasing frequency. Called by a variety of names, the most common term used nowadays is *flexible manufacturing system* (FMS). Development of these systems began in the late 1960s in Germany (both East and West), Japan, and the United States. A number of these systems or variations of them are in place in these countries at the present time. As the parts-producing plants of companies are being revamped or modernized, these systems are being chosen in preference to more conventional stand-alone machines.

The most convenient way to illustrate the FMS concept and to make clear the nature of its impact on the manufacturing organization is to use an actual prototypical example. Figure 2

is a drawing of an FMS introduced by Okuma Machinery
Works of Japan at the Chicago machine tool show in the early
1970s. It is an excellent example of the range of functions that
can be combined and the resulting versatility of such systems.
The Okuma Parts Center makes a variety of shaftlike parts of
the kind shown in Figure 3. These are cylindrical parts that
may have a number of steps of different diameters, and may
have flat surfaces or keyway slots milled into the cylindrical
surfaces. The system makes these finished, hardened, ground,
and inspected parts from metal rods that constitute the
machine's raw stock. Moreover, the system can make a number of different shafts in any predetermined sequence, automatically changing its operations, tools, and cutting se-
quences for each different part.

To manufacture parts on the Okuma system, metal rods of
varying diameter and composition are placed into a holding
mechanism that can rotate to position the correct stock for
feeding into an automatic turret lathe. Here the rough shape
of the part is formed and the piece is cut off the rod. The
workpiece is removed from the lathe by a robot arm that
moves the part to a machining center where any needed flat
surfaces and holes are milled and drilled. Then the part is
picked up by a robot arm and moved to an induction furnace
where its surface is hardened. Another robot arm removes the
hardened piece and places it into an automated inspection
station where measurements of the critical dimensions are
made. Then the arm moves the part to a cylindrical grinder
and finished surfaces are produced. After a second trip to the
inspection station for final checking, the workpiece moves by
conveyor out of the system. At no point in this process is there
human intervention. All the coordination of machine operation, tool selection, workpiece movement, and inspection is
handled by computer. Each machine in the system can be
busy on a differently designed part at the same time.

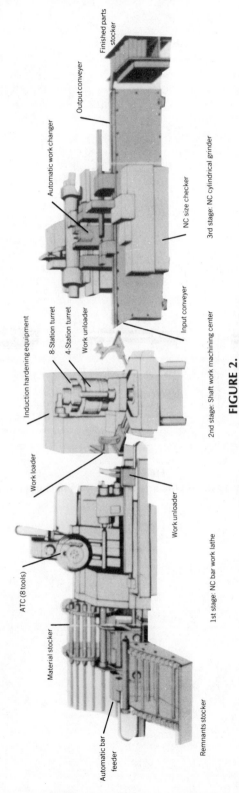

FIGURE 2.

Okuma Parts Center 1, Flexible Manufacturing System

Material stocker

ATC (8 tools)

Automatic bar feeder

Remnants stocker

Work unloader

1st stage: NC bar work lathe

Work loader

Induction hardening equipment

8-Station turret

4-Station turret

Work unloader

2nd stage: Shaft work machining center

Automatic work changer

Output conveyer

Finished parts stocker

NC size checker

Input conveyer

3rd stage: NC cylindrical grinder

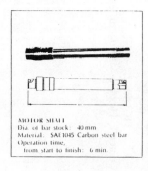

MOTOR SHAFT
Dia. of bar stock: 40 mm
Material: SAE1045 Carbon steel bar
Operation time,
from start to finish: 6 min.

GEAR SHAFT
Dia. of bar stock: 50 mm
Material: SAE1045 Carbon steel bar
Operation time,
from start to finish: 5 min. 50 sec.

SHAFT
Dia. of bar stock: 60 mm
Material: SAE1045 Carbon steel bar
Operation time,
from start to finish: 5 min. 30 sec.

FIGURE 3.
Typical Parts Made on Okuma Flexible Manufacturing System

The concept behind this FMS is the integration of all the machines and equipment needed to make a "family" of parts, in this case, shaftlike cylindrical parts. This principle of machine clustering, called Group Technology, recognizes that certain parts share common physical configurations that require essentially the same processing steps. By grouping the machines needed for these steps, much of the problem of transporting the workpieces, scheduling the machines, and accounting for the parts is greatly simplified. When the computer is used to integrate these process steps, the improvement is even more dramatic, because the time between steps can be reduced to seconds. Systems such as this have been set up to make gears, other forms of turned parts, and prismatic (flat-surfaced) parts. Some systems handle parts weighing hundreds of pounds.

What makes systems of this kind so important? Here are some of their major virtues:

Shortened throughput time

Once the system has been programmed to make a particular part, the setup time at each machine for that part is a matter of a few seconds while the workpiece is being automatically positioned and clamped and the proper tool is indexed into place. This extremely short setup time frees the manufacturer from the constraint of having to make parts in batches in order to spread the cost of setup over a sufficiently large number of pieces. When parts are made in batches, each piece in the batch must wait at each operation until every other piece in the batch has been processed. Only then is the batch moved to the next operation, where the waiting process is repeated.

In flexible manufacturing systems, parts can proceed individually from station to station without waiting. Throughput time (time it takes for a part to move from raw stock through to finished piece) is greatly shortened. To appreciate the enormous reduction in throughput time possible, consider the parts made on the Okuma system. If any of these parts were to be made in batches in a conventional job shop, they might take as long as 10 weeks to be completed and ready for assembly. This is in contrast to getting a completely finished part just 5 or 6 minutes after the system is commanded to produce the part and the proper raw stock is provided to the machine.

The key to the radical change in throughput time is the reduction in (1) setup time, because the computer knows what adjustments must be made by the machine and gives the commands for virtually instant change, and (2) transport time, because the robot moves the piece from one workstation to another in a few seconds. In a conventional metalworking shop, individual general purpose machines tend to be clustered by the type of operation they perform. Thus, there will be a milling department, a drilling department, a grinding department, a heat treating department, and so on. Machine setup for any single operation is done manually and may take from 15 minutes to several hours. With such a high cost of setup, it is impractical to produce just one part and then change to another setup. Instead, as many identical parts as can be economically justified are run through the operation at the same time, each part in the batch waiting for all the other parts to be worked on before the batch is moved to the next operation, where the process is repeated. Movement of the batches is also a manual task, and there are usually delays in notifying a materials handler and in getting the parts moved. Some shops of this kind have a general rule of thumb: "one week of throughput time for each operation." The nearly instantaneous setup and transport time of flexible manufacturing systems eliminates such delays. They also eliminate the need for the people who do the setups and transporting.

Reduced inventories

Shortened throughput time means greatly reduced work in process inventories. If it takes 10 weeks to complete parts, a plant must have 10 weeks of work out on the shop floor. If, instead, parts completion times are measured in minutes or hours, work in process shrinks to a matter of a few days, with consequent savings in capital tied up in inventory. This concept of reduced throughput time and inventory is one of the essential parts of the Japanese concept of "just-in-time" supply of parts in manufacture.[12]

Reduced labor cost

These systems effect enormous reductions in labor cost. As an illustration, consider that to duplicate the output of the Okuma system with conventional stand-alone machines, one would need at least the following labor complement:

1 lathe operator
1 milling machine operator
1 heat treat attendant
1 grinder attendant
1 inspector
1 setup person
1 materials handler

Each time a new part is to be processed through a conventional shop, a setup person is needed to position the correct holding fixtures and attach the proper cutting tools to do the job. (If machine operators are expected to perform their own setup operations, the capacity of the shop may be reduced.) When operations are performed on physically separate machines, as is done in a conventional arrangement, one operator is normally required at each machine—lathe, milling machine, grinder—loading and unloading parts, starting and stopping the machine, supervising machine functions, and generating production and quality control information. Heat treating to harden the surface of a part is usually handled in a location in the plant remote from machining operations, and one attendant may be in charge of several heat treating furnaces at the same time. Inspections may be needed at various points between process steps, and the need for materials handling will depend on the distances between each of the machining steps. In plants where machines are segregated by type, the distances may be great, and several handlers may be needed. The above list does not take into consideration the supervision or other support activities needed by this number of employees. This group of people and their machines might be able to produce about 80 percent of the output per shift of the FMS, which does not stop for breaks.

In contrast, the FMS requires only one operator to load materials and monitor the system. Of course, programming, tooling, and debugging labor is required whenever a new part is prepared for manufacture on the FMS, but this is a one-time effort for each part design, and a similar amount of work would be needed if the stand-alone machines had some form of programmable controls. Even more of this type of labor would be required for more conventional general-purpose machine tools. Maintenance labor would also be about equivalent, and there is the potential advantage under computer control that the maintenance mechanic can be aided by the computer in diagnosing the machine's ills.

Thus, the ratio of labor displaced by this particular system is at least 7:1 and could be as high as 9:1. We have seen systems where this ratio is 10:1, and G.E. has a system in their locomotive works at Erie, Pennsylvania, where the ratio is reported to be 30:1.[13] (Discussions with representatives from this plant indicate a significantly lower displacement ratio.) These numbers indicate why the 2:1 displacement ratio of a robot working alone is so much less potent an influence on labor displacement than is the computer-integrated manufacturing system.

Integration of coordinating and support functions

The time compression effected by the FMS removes any possibility of having any of the conventional manufacturing support infrastructure (Production Control, Dispatching, Expediting, Inventory Control, Quality Control, Material Handling) interact with the system in conventional ways at any of the steps within the process. This contrasts sharply with the traditional job shop, where the trick is to keep track of the jobs on the shop floor, keep them moving, check quality and yield, set priorities at each machine, and to make sure delivery commitments are met. These activities require the services of a number of specialists in organizationally separate support groups. Communications and response delays among these groups and between these groups and the line production organization account for a good part of the long throughput time experienced in conventional shops.

Because the computer accomplishes coordination tasks in seconds, and parts are dispatched to move from station to station automatically,in seconds or minutes, human coordination and support requirements are substantially reduced. This is another source of labor savings for computer-integrated systems that is not even included in the high displacement ratios previously mentioned.

Reduced importance of economies of scale

A manufacturer can now produce a relatively small number of parts of a given kind annually at costs that are competitive with those of high-volume mass production ("fixed automation") systems. Although not quite as efficient as the dedicated transfer line typical of automobile engine manufacture, the flexibility of these systems in adjusting to different products assures them of long useful lifetimes. When the part being made on a fixed automation transfer line is eliminated or substantially changed, the entire line must be torn down and rebuilt or scrapped. An FMS merely needs to be reprogrammed and, perhaps, retooled.

The implication is that economies of scale in discrete product manufacture may no longer be as great as they have been in conventional, noncomputerized operations. The smaller firm, or division of a larger firm, carefully structured to take advantage of computer-integrated manufacture, may be highly competitive with the industrial giant, both in cost and in flexible response to market signals for product change.

Little change in capital investment

Flexible manufacturing systems need not require appreciably more capital investment than would be needed for the equivalent capacity of conventional machines, particularly when inventory reductions and the higher utilization rates of these systems are taken into account. Most of the evidence for this statement comes from informal discussions with users. Published data to support this contention are scarce, because firms that have installed systems are reluctant (or unable) to make public their cost information. Also, many installations are of the "first-ever" variety, which entail more than usual design, installation, and start-up costs.

The FMS concept is a clear extension of the computer/telecommunications technology already exploited in the continuous process industries of chemicals, petroleum, utilities, and paper. As materials consistencies increase and as processes become more deterministic, computers will be able to take over the job of controlling systems of machines that multiply human productivity rather than simply replace it.

There is no reason, either, to limit the concept of computer integration to the family-of-parts FMS. These individual systems can become cells of higher levels of integration—networks of networks—tying together fabrication, finishing, and assembly systems in ways that ultimately approach the concept of the unmanned factory.

TELECOMMUNICATIONS

The evolution of electronic communications technology has been characterized by a series of technical and regulatory breakthroughs that have greatly expanded capabilities (speed, accuracy, capacity, noise reduction) and have cut cost. These breakthroughs have occurred despite the greater maturity and oligopolistic structure of the communications industry. The structural rigidity of this industry seems actually to have stimulated firms outside the industry to develop technical alternatives to conventional systems, and this, in turn, has led to regulatory changes that have opened business opportunities for competing modes.

The elemental breakthrough in telecommunications technology is computer-derived: the digitization of electronic signals. As the cost of converting signals into coded pulses dropped with the advent of solid state circuitry, it became economic to digitize all forms of information for transmission and for processing. When an analog signal such as a temperature reading is converted to a digital signal, the information needed to reproduce that reading can be transmitted great distances with little error or loss of information. It can be compressed into much narrower bandwidths and shorter transmission times. Also, the digitized signal can be handled or exchanged among a variety of terminals, processors, or actuators. The conversion of voice and other analog signals into digital form has established a common signal format, making innovations in transmission techniques possible.

Transmission technology has been undergoing radical change over the past two decades. Three significant developments account for most of the change:

1. Ground-based and satellite microwave transmission systems.
2. Local area networks.
3. Optical fiber transmission.

Line-of-sight microwave and video signal transmission has been a common technology for many years. As conventional copper wire transmission systems have become crowded, noisy, and undependable for massive data flows, microwave links have been established, but primarily for fairly short distances. Television relay links of this sort have also been used for both private and public communication. A major step forward in microwave technology came with the commercial geosynchronous satellite, greatly increasing the effective range of microwave transmission. Now all parts of the world can be reached instantly and at a low cost per message. With satellite transmission, cost is no longer a function of distance.

Distance has been only one of the problems overcome by new telecommunications technology. The volume of communications in modern large organizations has become so great that conventional telephone lines and written messages fail to meet the needs. Firms have been in danger of choking on their ever-mounting information load. Several companies, including Xerox and GTE, have introduced new methods to deal with the problem. Exploiting the principle that all forms of communication can be digitized, these firms have developed and marketed local area telecommunication networks, in which there is a common high capacity "bus" or linkage for all communications, whether computer data, word processing, voice, or machine operating instructions. These networks allow computers to talk to computers, computers to machines, typing terminals to computers, computers to printers, and people to people. These networks solve the problem of communications capacity.

The third technological breakthrough in transmission systems uses light pulses sent through optical fibers. In advanced fiber optic systems the light is generated by lasers, coded as a digitized signal and carried through ultrapure glass fibers at very low transmission losses. Optical fibers have very broad bandwidths, meaning that they can each carry enormous amounts of data, far more than can be achieved by conventional copper telephone wires. One pair of hairlike fibers can carry at least 1300 simultaneous telephone conversations. In contrast, only 24 conversations can be handled by a pair of copper wires. A single cable containing 144 fibers will carry up to 240,000 conversations, twice that of a copper cable having roughly 20 times the cross-sectional area. Optical fibers can also carry television signals, making it possible to provide video, computer, and voice communication through the single medium. Such systems are much more secure from eavesdropping, and they are also impervious to electromagnetic noise interference both inside and outside the factory. A long-distance link using cables of bundled optical fibers was recently put into use between New York and Washington D.C. The 372-mile link is the largest optical fiber transmission system yet installed. It will be extended to reach from Cambridge, Massachusetts to Moseley, Virginia. A similar line is in progress in California; it is planned to extend from Sacramento to San Diego.[14] A trans-Atlantic fiber optic cable is due to be in operation by 1988, and we may expect gradual displacement of copper wires and cables by buried optical fiber cables over the next two decades.

The import of these technical developments is that we are now able to transmit enormous quantities of information, including the massive data banks built up by computers, over any amount of distance, virtually error-free and at reasonable cost.

CONVERGENCE

The stage is thus set for the third act of this technical drama—the convergence of computer and telecommunications technologies. We saw that the evolution of computer applications in manufacturing was toward integration, where more and more processes are brought under coordinated computer management. Such systems may have distributed networks of computers, in which low-level microprocessors or programmable controllers may manage only one function or operation, while other larger computers manage larger sections of the system and coordinate information flows throughout the system. Such complex interrelationships require real-time, low-error computer-to-computer communication. Telecommunications technology is now ready to handle the job.

Because the computer/telecommunications marriage is only now being consummated, it is a little early to predict all the forms of new technology that will be spawned. There is no doubt that the offspring will be many and varied. We have already seen telephones that act as computers and computers that act as telephones, newspapers, and mail systems. Changes occurring in financial systems in this country provide excellent examples of the combined power of computer and telecommunications technology. There is an integration of functions, oriented heavily toward market segments. Conventional transactions with many customers are moving toward paperless electronic funds transfers and accounting. In these systems the volume of transactions has increased manifold in the last decade, and the capacities of computers and communications systems have had to stretch to meet the demand. Conversely, the demand for human "transactions processors" has declined. In one major financial institution the volume of transactions has increased fourfold in the past decade, but personnel handling these transactions have declined from 8500 to 6500. Exemplifying the concept of networks of networks, the Electronic Funds Transfer Association recently announced that at least seven nationwide networks of automated bank teller machine systems were in operation or were about to go into operation. One network will connect 35 banking institutions and 10,000 banking machines.[15]

The same proliferation of convergent technologies will be occurring in manufacturing. Signs of these changes can already be seen. In continuous process factories we already have remote monitoring of processes, aided by video screens and computer information processing. We also have early installations of systems that respond to a limited range of voice commands. Local area networks are now being extended and interconnected, producing "nets of nets," stretching across the country, across the globe, and even surmounting such traditional barriers as those between engineering and production departments of the same firm. Computer integration of design, engineering, manufacturing process control, and testing has already begun, resulting in savings in labor and shorter product lead times. Computer-based systems of planning, material control, and procurement are not only able to communicate among various plants or locations in a plant but also with the computers of suppliers and of customers.

3

OTHER EMERGING TECHNOLOGIES

Computers and telecommunications are not the only principles, of course, that are fueling technological change in industry today. There are many techniques being employed that are bringing about new and useful results. Laser, electron beam, plasma, and acoustic technologies have a wide range of application. Pattern recognition technologies are giving machines the ability to see and to act more intelligently. New materials have become available. The high cost of energy has encouraged many diverse attempts to develop new energy sources or to increase efficiency of use. Finally, the rapid growth in understanding of genetic principles has brought us to the threshold of a new world of biotechnology, in which human well-being will be enhanced by the engineering of living matter.

How do these technologies fit into the overall picture of future manufacturing technology? In general, there is a mutually supporting relationship between these other emerging technologies and the major computer/telecommunications technologies. In some instances, a particular technique is an essential ingredient in making the computer or telecommunications technologies possible. Lasers that generate the light used to carry signals in optical fibers have this kind of role in advanced telecommunications technology. In other cases, as in pattern recognition, the technique is highly dependent on computer control or telecommunication support to make it feasible for production use. Because of this close interdependence, it will be useful to describe briefly each of these other technologies.

LASERS (COHERENT LIGHT)

Laser light is emitted as a single frequency with its wave fronts all in phase. Radiation of this kind is called "coherent." Such light has unusual properties. It can be focused to an extremely fine point, it can be shaped into a narrow pencil beam that retains its shape in the atmosphere over many miles, it can be pulsed, and it bounces along inside optical glass fibers with little loss of energy. High-power lasers allow for the transmission of large amounts of clean energy in highly concentrated form.

The laser device is well established and increasing in useful applications as its performance characteristics are broadened and as its cost decreases. Lasers have been used to generate localized heating for cutting, drilling, welding, and marking solid materials. They are used, for instance, for cutting and drilling ceramics and similar hard, brittle materials, for precision trimming of hairlike wires on microelectronic components, or for welding steel plates as thick as 3/8 inch. Because the beam can pass through a transparent medium, items to be cut or welded can be placed inside a vacuum chamber in which there is a window for the beam.

The narrow, straight laser beam is used in inspection for checking dimensions and surfaces. It is used in aligning tools accurately in machines, and in aligning machines on the production floor. Fiber optic laser sensors are able to measure pressure, temperature, acceleration, rotation, strain, and electric and magnetic fields, so they have the potential of informing process control computers about the condition of many different processes. Laser beams are used for high-density recording of information (optical data storage) and for high-speed character formation for printing. Chemical reactions in extremely small quantities of material can be produced by laser heating. Medical uses of lasers in treatment of disease and in surgery are common, and military uses range from laser aiming and range-finding devices to directed energy weapons systems.[16]

In virtually all of these uses the laser has been, in effect, a tool. Its unique properties have provided opportunities for applications in many areas, but each application is rather circumscribed. Users of the devices in each of these applications number in the hundreds or thousands, not in the millions. This is true in manufacturing uses just as it is in medicine, surveying, or the military.

It is possible, however, that the new field of optical electronics may give the laser a much more pervasive influence. Optical microcircuits analogous to electronic microcircuits are being developed for computer use. Microsized lasers are the sources of light that can be switched off and on in picoseconds (millionths of a millionth of a second) by indium antimonide crystal switches. This is as much as a thousand times faster than microelectronic transistor switches.[17] In this form of application lasers are likely to become microcircuit components and become integral parts of the ever-expanding computer/telecommunications combination. Although adding to the speed and capacity of these systems, laser technology in this form would have little independent impact on manufacturing.

ELECTRON BEAM AND PLASMA TECHNOLOGY

The most common electron beam is that which produces the picture in a video tube or the display on a computer terminal.

These are relatively low-power beams. High-energy electron beams have been used for a number of years in metal welding and cutting. Electron beams provide very high heat concentrations—as great as are produced in conventional electric arc welding. The welds are clean and concentrated. A vacuum chamber is required, however, which makes this a difficult process for high-volume manufacturing or for very large pieces. It is particularly useful for welding metals (such as titanium) that are subject to atmospheric contamination.[18]

Plasmas are a state of matter that can be described as highly ionized gases, that is, the parts of a gas molecule carry positive or negative charges of electricity and are in a highly excited state. Plasmas can conduct great quantities of electrical energy, and their most common manufacturing application is in cutting and welding. Plasma arcs, in which a gas such as argon is injected into the arc itself, are, like electron beams, characterized by high temperature and concentration of energy. Among other applications, plasma arcs are used for applying metal coatings to base metals.

Both electron beam and plasma technologies have the advantage of being easily automated and computer controlled. Not only can the beam or arc itself be controlled accurately, but workplace holding fixtures under computer control can be rotated and translated to permit continuous welding or cutting of complex shapes.

Because of their high processing speeds and ease of automation, electron beam and plasma technology will continue to grow in application during the decade, selectively displacing older, more conventional forms of cutting and welding. Because laser welding requires no special provision for vacuum, it is possible that this will become the more dominant future welding technology, supplanting conventional and electron beam methods.

ACOUSTICS

Sound energy, audible and ultrasonic, is finding increased use in industrial applications. Ultrasonic devices have been used for years in connection with cleaning the surfaces of objects, bonding materials such as plastics or paper, and for grinding a variety of materials. Ultrasonic systems are also being used to detect subsurface flaws or hidden structures in materials.

Acoustic technology is becoming a useful noninvasive, non-contact means of inspecting solid parts. Coupled with pattern recognition technology, acoustic inspection methods provide rapid in-process checks that can materially aid computer-based automated systems. In related applications, acoustic sensors can pick up machine noises and transmit them to analytical devices that can interpret these noises as signs of bearing wear, lack of lubricant, or failed parts.

As with most of the technical principles we investigated, acoustic devices in manufacturing are not a major force. They are a facilitating influence for automation, however, and they add to the momentum of computer-based technology in changing the nature of manufacturing and the character of work.

PATTERN RECOGNITION

Pattern recognition is a phenomenon of the computer. It is a software technology that enables machines to "see" or to "hear" information and to process the information so they can act on it. Vision systems are being used to assist robots in selecting workpieces and correctly orienting them. Other vision systems are being used to inspect microelectronic chips and integrated circuits. Early vision systems were employed to read letter and number characters. Optical character readers (OCRs) are being used by banks and other institutions requiring rapid processing of thousands of similar documents. Word processing systems employing OCRs are also available.

Speech recognition systems with limited vocabularies and tolerances for different speakers have been used in manufacturing operations where simple grading ("good," "bad," "rework") or go/no-go instructions are all that is required to activate a machine to perform a task.

Vision systems tend to rely on vidicon (television type) cameras or charge-coupled device (solid state photosensitive component) arrays for image acquisition; the pattern recognition processing is done by computer. Audio signals, converted to digitized electronic signals, are likewise processed by computer. Because of the large, complex software programs used in most pattern recognition approaches, this field is basically a specialized branch of computer technology.

Vision and speech recognition systems are expected to evolve slowly during the coming decade. Devices used in manufacturing need to be rugged, reliable, and versatile, and these systems are still having problems in the manufacturing environment. High cost has been another factor. Certain routine high-volume tasks in which human error levels are unacceptable may be prime targets for specialized pattern recognition techniques. Inspection of the thousands of microscopic components on an integrated circuit chip that is being made by the hundreds of thousands is that kind of task. In such instances, pattern recognition systems have the potential for very high gains in productivity. What may take a person hours to inspect can be processed by a computer-based system in a fraction of a second. Because of the tedious nature of such chores, the error level of the computer-based system is likely to be much lower than can be achieved by human inspectors.

MATERIALS INNOVATIONS

Radical changes in manufacturing need not be confined to processes. The materials being used can also change. Although most of our attention in our study focused on the processes that were being derived from basic technical principles, we inquired about materials and the changes envisioned for them in the coming decade.

Three trends in materials were evident:

Development of new materials or new applications for uncommon materials to satisfy extraordinary performance requirements

Applications calling for high strength and corrosion resistance at high temperatures, for example, have resulted in the use of titanium and ceramics in jet engines and rocket components. Light weight and high strength requirements have encouraged the adoption of graphite composite (graphite fibers in an epoxy matrix) materials in such diverse areas as aircraft structural components, tennis rackets, and bicycle frames. New techniques for depositing special coatings on metal, ceramic, and plastic surfaces have greatly expanded the range of materials applications. Various coatings provide hardness, chemical and corrosion resistance, lubricity, conductivity, wear resistance, and aesthetic appeal.

Selection of substitute materials made necessary by changes in prices, technical needs, or recognition of social hazards

Where easy substitution has been possible, as was the case in the early 1970s when aluminum was substituted for copper in response to higher copper prices, the changes occur within only a few years and change back when prices reverse. The development of ultrapure optical fibers for high-density information transmission is an example of materials substitution for technical reasons, in this case to overcome the capacity limitations of copper cable. Substitutes for asbestos are being sought to replace what has become recognized as a cause of a form of lung cancer.

Use of recycled materials, driven by the economics of scarcity

At the same time that large integrated steel mills in the United States have been struggling for survival, the so-called mini-mills that use scrap steel as a raw material have been flourishing. Recovery and re-use of copper, lead, aluminum, petroleum-based solvents, and paper continues to grow.

When new materials are introduced into a product, the processes that make the product are likely to change also. Graphite composites provide an excellent example. Not only are the processes for producing graphite fibers and epoxy different from those needed to produce aluminum or titanium, but the process of laying up, cutting, curing, finishing, and testing is entirely different from metal forming, heat treating, and assembly. Similar changes will be experienced if a ceramic engine block design replaces the conventional cast iron block in the automobile, or if optical fibers replace copper telephone lines and video cables.

Although materials innovations are undoubtedly going to continue, technologists tend to agree that there will be no materials changes having widespread impact during in the next 10 years. The picture appears to be one of incremental change in one application after another, with the overall effect being a very gradual shift in the composition of our products.

OTHER TECHNOLOGIES

The foregoing discussions do not exhaust the list of emergent technologies. Given the myriad scientific and technical principles on which new technologies can be based, it would be difficult and unproductive to attempt a complete enumeration. In our discussions with corporate technologists we did consider these other areas:

Light holography

The use of laser-generated coherent light to record and reproduce three-dimensional images. Some application of this principle is being used in industry for the inspection of parts.

Superconductivity

The electrical resistance of certain materials at extremely low temperatures becomes zero, thus permitting small conductor wires to carry very large currents. This principle is being applied in making magnets with very strong magnetic fields. Experimental superconductive electric power generators are being developed, and some designs of nuclear fusion reactors depend on superconductive coils to produce the magnetic fields needed to contain the reaction. Nuclear magnetic resonance systems that rely on superconducting coils are now being used experimentally to detect chemical concentrations within the human body, a process considered superior in several ways to X-ray diagnosis. Limited applications of superconductivity may begin to show up in manufacturing in future decades.

An array of principles used in materials forming

These include powder metallurgy, near-net-shape forging, electric discharge machining, electrochemical machining, high energy rate forming, extrusion, casting, molding, punching, and pressing. Innovations in each of these fields tend to be in specialized niches, rather than of general use.

Continuing improvement and new applications are likely to be found with regard to all of these processes, but progress is expected to be gradual. All the changes in these areas taken together will have only a slight effect on the economics or structure of American manufacturing during the next decade, and their general impact on human resources in manufacturing will also be minor.

BIOTECHNOLOGY

Biotechnology is a different matter. This is an emerging technology that will have an important and lasting impact on workforces and on our way of life. Technologists readily acknowledge the future importance of enzyme technology, genetic engineering, and other forms of manipulating living cells in production processes. Several of the companies that we interviewed were engaged in various aspects of biological product and process development. Representatives of these companies and those in other companies that were monitoring developments were unanimous, however, in their opinion that manufacturing applications of the current experimental work would not occur in any appreciable way in the next decade. Except for those firms that are trying to be on the leading edge of the biotechnical field, the manufacturing implications are so distant that they fall outside normal corporate planning horizons. People charged with devising corporate strategies for coping with imminent technological change generally will not need to be concerned with the impacts of biotechnologies now. Those involved with long-term product and process technology strategy, however, will be well advised if they keep developments in these potentially important future technologies continuously in view.

SUMMARY

The essence of what we have said thus far about future manufacturing technology is this:

The paramount development overshadowing all other technological changes in manufacturing for at least the next decade will be the integration of manufacturing processes and information into automated productive systems through massive use of low-cost computers and high-capacity communication networks. The global view, from the vantage point of the manufacturing industry, is that we are entering the time when these two extremely useful, broadly applicable technologies are merging. Compared with the influence of computers and telecommunications on manufacturing, all other emerging technical principles fade into the background or join, as supporting technologies, into the integration process.

Of greatest importance is the immense breadth of application of these two technologies. From a national viewpoint this factor is much more significant than the pace with which the changes will occur. It is unlikely that there will be overnight conversion of whole industries to the new computer/telecommunications technologies. In fact, the change process will continue to be evolutionary, but spurred by the pressures of competition and costs. What makes these technologies so important is that they are *universal*; they apply in all industries. Their effects, therefore, will be enormous, because they will be experienced in all sectors.

A less global view would recognize that many of the other technologies have important niches in future manufacturing processes. The human consequences of their adoption, even for the firms in which the niches exist, however, are not likely to provoke widespread concern, nor is it likely that industry-level strategies will be needed to deal with them.

4

IMPLICATIONS OF EVOLVING TECHNOLOGY

General Effects on the Firm

We have stated that the introduction of new manufacturing technologies is an evolutionary process, but certain changes in business organization, practice, and strategy will be required to implement the new technology successfully. These changes may justifiably be considered the seeds that produce a cultural revolution. There will be widespread changes in the structure and management of industrial firms, changes in the optimal scale and timing of production and allied activities, and even more fundamentally, changes in the way people think about such concepts as manufacturing processes, firms, and industries.

Our primary concern is to examine the probable effects of computer/telecommunications technologies on the workforce. It will be easier to understand the nature of the impacts on people, however, after we have first considered how these technologies will change firms themselves.

When computer/telecommunications technologies are introduced into manufacturing firms, they will affect the pattern and pace of production, inventories, product strategies, firm size, organizational structure, and interfirm relationships. These changes, in turn, will have an important bearing on the size and nature of the workforce. The relative ease and speed with which production processes can be optimized or changed completely will have a profound effect on the way firms use their production capabilities to create new strategies with respect to their markets, suppliers, and inventories. The impact of new technology on production will extend well beyond the manufacturing process itself, upstream to the design and development functions of the firm and to its materials supply systems, and downstream to product distribution and marketing. Radical changes in any one of these areas would be sufficient to make significant differences in a firm's operations. Simultaneous changes in all these areas could produce a radically altered business. As we shall see later, the nature of work and the workforce is also likely to change, so there is little that is basic to the functions of the firm that will be unaffected by computer/telecommunications technology.

It is essential when we consider the effects of computer and communications technologies in manufacturing that we address all industry, not just special parts of it. These technologies are general. That is what makes them so very important. They are not specific or limited, such as the continuous casting process in steelmaking or the float process for glass. Important as these more specific technologies may be, they apply only to a single industry or part of a single industry.

We have said that the introduction of computer/communications technology is similar to the introduction of the electric motor into industry. That, too, was universal in scope. There is, however, an important difference. The electric motor could not generate, distribute, analyze, or act on information. Until this latest technological revolution only humans could do that. This qualitative difference substantially alters the nature of the effects that can be expected.

TIME HORIZONS

New computer-based technology can cut the time required to introduce new products. At the same time that a new product or part is being designed, instructions for the production process to make that item can be generated. The machines needed, the raw materials and tools required, and the machine operations can all be specified and programmed. All of this occurs in the form of computerized data that are immediately available for production start-up.

Traditionally, firms have maintained a rather formal separation between design departments and production units.
Reasons for this vary, but a part of the rationale has been the
need for an explicit "buying off" of a design by the manufacturing team at the time of product design release. The organizational and procedural distances thus established have meant
that the transfer process has been slow, often adversarial in
nature, and expensive in terms of time involvement of key
personnel in the organization. Access to up-to-date information has been limited to the number of copies of paper documents that could be distributed; and, because changes have
taken days to document, there has always been the danger
that production or procurement units would be operating on
the basis of old, incorrect information. Computer assistance
in design and design transfer cuts out the large time lags
between design and manufacture and makes information
much more generally and immediately available. One technologist we interviewed described a change of this type in his
firm in this way:

> It used to be [you would] just take the basic data, program it,
> run a tape, put the tape in a numerically controlled machine
> and you'd run it. Then we went to direct numerical control,
> where we're programming and going directly into the ma-
> chine and driving it by the computer rather than by the tape.
> Now we're taking that next step—making it a fluid operation.
> As [a part] is designed it is taken right into the programming
> process and the programmers are programming and driving
> the machine. They can program an image upstairs and then go
> downstairs and [a machine will produce the part] for you.

The rapid transition from product design to production to
marketing means that the scheduling of new product introduction collapses to intervals that are quite short in comparison to those experienced in the recent past. One result of the

foreshortening of time horizons for product introduction or change is improved system efficiency, which translates into lower overhead and lower product cost. Another result is an enhanced ability to produce altered or "customized" versions of a product or even entirely new products quickly and at competitive cost. In recent years, General Motors has surprised even itself at how fast major auto configuration changes could be accomplished through computer-aided design of product and process and through computer-aided transfer of designs into manufacturing.

Time horizons are also collapsing in those industries that do not design and manufacture discrete products, but instead are involved in continuous manufacturing operations (petroleum refining, pulp and paper, chemicals, primary metals, etc.). Now that computers are able to capture and analyze enormous quantities of data generated in continuous production, these data may be used to model the process, so potential alterations can be simulated in detail by the computer. The process can thus be brought to optimal conditions quickly and accurately.

The successful firm of the future will have the capability for rapidly changing or adjusting its production systems. The computer's ability to monitor processes more closely and continuously makes it possible to set process parameters (flow rates, temperatures, pressures, dimensions, basis weight, etc.) more precisely without excessive trial-and-error approaches. One continuous process manufacturer, for example, told us that the new microprocessor-controlled machines being installed in one of his firm's facilities would essentially permit them to "dial up" the desired type of output. These machines are sufficiently flexible to permit hourly changes in product type, if necessary, to satisfy customer needs or take advantage of market opportunities.

INVENTORIES

A major element in the justification for capital expenditures for computer-integrated systems is the reduction in inventory investment that can be achieved.

When new or specialized goods can be produced at lower cost and with less conversion time, the optimal size of production runs is reduced. Currently, for most manufacturers, it is substantially more expensive to produce a variety of "made-to-order" goods than it is to make large quantities of a few relatively standard items and maintain large inventories from which to fill orders. The decrease in lead time needed for production start-up and the shorter throughput time made possible by computer/telecommunications technologies will make it profitable for firms to offer a greater proportion of their products as made-to-order goods.

Even those firms that deliver goods from inventory will be able to maintain substantially smaller work-in-process and finished-goods inventories than in the past. Work-in-process inventories are goods that are being worked on that have not yet reached finished product state. The size of a firm's work-in-process inventory is determined by the value of the inputs (materials, labor, overhead) into the product and by the length of time it takes to complete the production process. For any given product, cutting throughput time in half is tantamount to cutting work-in-process inventory in half. The introduction of computer-integrated manufacturing systems has been able to effect substantially greater throughput time reductions than that. Consider the parts made on the Okuma parts center described in Chapter 2. If these parts were to take 6 weeks to go through a conventional machine shop, a reduction to 6 minutes throughput time involves a work-in-process inventory reduction of over 99.9%!

Finished-goods inventory levels are largely dependent on customer requirements and competitive pressures. Inventory size is a tradeoff between the costs of having an inventory from which to satisfy customer demand—costs that include warehousing, spoilage, obsolescence, and investment carrying costs—and the costs of not having inventory, which can include customer dissatisfaction, loss of sales, and production start-up and expediting costs. An important factor in inventory size is the lead time required to replenish depleted stocks. If customers can be served satisfactorily from a reduced inventory because the process responds swiftly to changes in customer demand, then finished goods inventory can be reduced. Fast response is one of the features of computer-integrated manufacturing technology, and advanced telecommunications merely enhances this capability by providing nearly instantaneous communications from buyers, sales people, and test markets.

The same forces at work in final-goods manufacturing firms will also affect their suppliers. Supplier firms will be able to respond more rapidly to changes in the demand for their products, and to supply new components with substantially reduced lead times. Suppliers that remain competitive will be able to meet these expectations. Computer networks in some firms, for example, now connect to those of their suppliers to cut lead times and reduce uncertainty. As suppliers reliably meet these challenges, their customer firms will alter their own behavior to take advantage of this new capability. Smaller stocks of raw materials and component parts will be maintained by manufacturing firms because the risk of being caught without an adequate supply of any particular input will be diminished.

PRODUCT LIFE-CYCLES

Product life-cycles will be shortened in many industries. We have witnessed this phenomenon in the microelectronics industry over the last decade. The integration of design and manufacturing through the use of computer/telecommunications techniques will reduce the costs of creating a new product. Even the time factors will be significantly reduced. Because the production processes will have become more adaptable and programmable it will be technically feasible and economical to follow changes in market demand quickly. Companies will now be in a position to pursue product strategies involving shorter product life-cycles, or to offer custom-made products for individual customer needs. Change in the nature of goods produced will become a more continuous process. At present it is a series of abrupt discontinuities.

A number of observers have recently emphasized the importance of flexibility in manufacturing, most recently in the context of comparisons with successful Japanese firms. Historically the ability to implement radical changes has been most closely associated with young firms or productive units that are generally small in size. Abernathy and Utterback have hypothesized that producers move through early phases of rapid product and process innovation, but often settle into a pattern of relatively little product change, and only incremental process innovation.[19] One of the keys to competitive success in the future will be the ability to shake off the addiction to incremental process innovation and to develop mechanisms that permit the introduction of relatively radical process and product innovations when there is a need for change. A similar thesis has been proposed by Klein.[20] He argues that those factors that lead firms to be very good at making incremental product changes also make it very difficult for them to react to major competitive threats from relatively radical product or process improvements.

Along this same line of thought, Abernathy, Clark, and Kantrow have recently argued that in many manufacturing industries the rapidly changing economic and competitive environment in which firms operate has resulted in a need to shift from small incremental innovations that are easily implemented in production processes to more dramatic changes that will require continuing adaptation of current and future manufacturing systems. As a result, they claim that it will be increasingly necessary to design flexibility into production processes to permit rapid adoption of future innovations.[21]

Reich extends this idea by stating that the successful American firm of the future will be the flexible firm, not the mass producer that has been the foundation of our industrial strength.[22] These ideas were shown to apply to the automotive industry in a recent National Academy of Engineering Report. This report notes that until recently, a principal theme in the history of the automobile industry has been a continuing process of increasing standardization, first of engines, then of chassis and of other components. The authors point out that this situation was reversed in the 1970s, and that more significant changes are to be expected in the future:

> The pattern of technical development suggests that innovation is becoming less incremental in its impact on the production unit. Recent changes have not just refined existing ideas but have also introduced new concepts; downsizing, trans-axles, and new materials are examples. Future technologies carry the possibility of significant change in production facilities; advanced engine concepts, materials and control systems that require radically different equipment, skills and organization.[23]

The problem of inflexibility in mass production methods has existed since the earliest days of their introduction. Hounshell argues that it was Leander McCormick's concern over the inflexibility of modern production techniques that explains why they were not adopted in the McCormick reaper factory before 1880. McCormick believed that his competitive advantage came from the ability to make frequent product changes, an option that was not then available under the new system.[24]

The advantages of greater production flexibility would be theoretical advantages and nothing more if it were not for the programmable capabilities of computer-managed machines. Flexibility, adaptability, and quick response are key features of computer-based technology. It is no accident that the need for flexibility is now being stressed. It is technically possible, it is a competitive weapon, and it will increasingly become a competitive necessity.

ECONOMIES OF SCALE

In our discussions with corporate technologists, we inquired about the implications of computer/telecommunications technologies regarding economies of scale and optimal plant size. This issue is important because achieving greater scale economies has been a road often traveled by firms in search of greater productivity and growth. Discussions of economies of scale have often led to confused and at times contradictory conclusions because of a tendency to confound a number of separate but related concepts. It is useful to define four separate categories of economies of scale. These are:

1. Economies of scale in productive unit size.
2. Economies of scale in production run size.
3. Economies of scale in plant size.
4. Economies of scale in firm size.

First, the term "economies of scale" most often refers to the decrease in unit costs that may be achieved by increases in the scale at which an individual production process in a particular plant is operated. In a paper mill, for example, one method of achieving economies of scale is to increase the width of the roll of paper handled by the papermaking machine. In this manner, the output of the machine may be increased without a proportional increase in cost.

In continuous-process manufacturing industries, increases in productive unit size have historically been the premier factor in productivity growth. Our interviews indicate that the scale of the productive unit is still increasing in these industries and is likely to continue to do so over the next decade. Some managers with whom we spoke, however, were concerned that the rate of productivity growth due to increases in productive unit size may slow in coming years as available economies become thoroughly exploited. Hence, a greater proportion of future productivity growth in these industries may stem from the savings that result from computer-based integration of the various functions of the firm, including further applications of computer control and telecommunications assistance to increase yields and reduce input costs.

In discrete manufacturing industries it is clear that process mechanization, introduced over the past century, has increased productivity through increased size of the productive unit. Much of this is due to the evolution from manual craft work to mechanized production line and the rationalization of work. More recently, however, process innovation that has led to productivity growth has not resulted in dramatic increases in the scale of production of the kind that were seen earlier. In our interviews with managers of discrete manufacturing facilities, we found very few that talked in terms of increasing productivity through a continuing scale-up in the size of production lines.

Even where the optimal size of production units continues to increase (as appears to be the case in a substantial portion of continuous process manufacturing industries), it does not necessarily follow that the optimal size of production runs will increase as well. Normally, increases in production run size would be expected to accompany increases in production unit size. However, the advent of computer-based automation introduces changes in this situation. Wherever the "make-ready" costs for a given production run are a substantial fraction of the total cost of the run, a significant reduction of these initial costs could mean that it is less costly to make smaller batches, even if the machines are larger. Better, more consistent yields also reduce production costs and make shorter production runs feasible. Customers are pressing for more specialized, "custom-made" products. This tends to push product manufacturing in the direction of shorter production runs. Furthermore, greater emphasis on just-in-time deliveries of materials and components will also tend to push supplier-manufacturers in the same direction.

These changes do not repeal the principle of economies of scale. Even very flexible automated systems will have lower unit costs for larger runs. The cost differential between smaller and larger batches, however, will have shrunk. In some instances the differential will be so small that other cost factors, such as the carrying cost of inventory, will mean that the overall cost of the product made in smaller batches is, indeed, lower. In other cases, the desire to provide rapid response to customer demand will make the firm indifferent to a modest difference in cost.

At this point, there is a mixture of trends relative to productive unit size and run size, depending on the industry. In steelmaking we see a trend toward smaller productive units, due to a technological shift toward electric arc furnaces and smaller run sizes. In petroleum refining, both the productive unit and the run size are increasing. In papermaking, the productive unit size is increasing, but, at least for the newer computer-integrated units, the run size is decreasing.

Turning to the question of optimal plant size, it must be noted that in many industries a typical factory of the future will have multiple production lines. That is, there will be several independent, identical or nearly identical production systems operating within a plant at any given time. These arrangements will develop because of a need to be able to produce a mix of products continuously, or because of a need to have redundant facilities to reduce the impact of equipment failure. In some instances, multiple production units represent the only way to achieve a level of capacity needed at that location. The units will be grouped together because of economies of materials availability, transportation, or services such as maintenance. The factors that determine optimal plant size, therefore, will be different from the factors that determine optimal production unit size.

When materials availability and costs are major factors for the commodity producer, transportation costs for both raw materials and finished product become very important. Paper and pulp manufacturing plant sizes tend to be limited, for example, by their proximity to harvestable timberlands and to their customers. The availability of labor in a given location may be a similar constraint on plant size.

Two newer ideas on plant size emerged in our interviews with manufacturing executives. The first is that some firms are experiencing a regionalization of their markets within the United States. Product requirements in one region differ from those in another, and larger firms are tailoring their production facilities and locations to become more responsive to these regional differences. The building products industry is one example where regional differences are important, but we found that parts of the chemical and petrochemical industries are also adjusting to this phenomenon.

Other firms are setting size limits for plants not in terms of physical capacity but in terms of numbers of people. For them, effective organizational size is the limiting criterion. Ease of communication, stronger interpersonal relationships, greater ability to motivate members, and the less formal organizational hierarchies possible with smaller populations are given as reasons for curtailing plant size. Many corporations have also changed their attitudes toward high community visibility strategies. There was a time when companies liked to be known as major employers in a particular area, but the political fallout from severe layoffs and plant closings has caused many firms to re-think this policy. For similar reasons, local governments are becoming increasingly wary of relying on a single employer to support their economy. One major electronics manufacturer told us that in his firm there is now a company policy against starting production facilities with more than 500 employees, and in no case are facilities to be allowed to increase beyond 1000 employees. We suspect that many industries will experience a growing trend toward smaller plants. This trend will be accentuated as improved communication links make geographically close ties with central corporate facilites less important and as more and more of the central functions are distributed to manufacturing installations.

Some traditional views of firm size have held that there are economies of scale completely separate from those of production unit size, production run size, or plant size. In part, these economies have involved service functions that are performed by the central corporation for a set of distributed manufacturing plants producing a range of products. Typical corporate services include research and development, economic planning, asset management, and legal services. There has been a recent trend toward greater disaggregation of research and development within firms, principally in an effort to put researchers in closer contact with customers, suppliers, and internal marketing staff. Our interviews have shown that more and more of the production data analysis and decision-making is being moved out of central headquarters as well. To the extent that this trend is a move toward essentially autonomous decentralized units within a corporate frame, the argument for larger firms on the basis of economies of scale is weakened. In some industries, at least, we may see a reversal of the tendency toward corporate gigantism.

Even where economies of firm size prevail it is clear that the new technologies will force changes in corporate strategy if the firm wishes to remain competitive in its markets. One manufacturing vice president told us that he believed that his firm, and United States industry in general, are going to have to move in the direction of looking more like today's high technology industries. He suggested that firms would have to shift to a "constant dynamic" mode where past perceptions of stability will no longer be either desirable or obtainable. Specifically, firms would be constantly involved in product changes driven by customer needs and competition. In this vice president's view, the idea of declining innovation in maturing industries, as has been described by Abernathy and Utterback, will have to change.

Will it be possible for large firms in the future to compete successfully with smaller firms when the crucial elements to success involve flexibility in design, production, and marketing? We do not have sufficient evidence to answer this question, but the evidence we do have counsels against national policies that view larger firms and mergers as the only strategy to cope with international competition. Smaller firms will have a very important role in providing fast response and innovative products for world markets.[25]

DECENTRALIZATION

As was indicated in the previous section, we see a diminishing of the size and importance of centralized corporate headquarters. More and more decision-making is being made on a decentralized basis, data analysis is being performed locally for immediate production optimization, and certain accounting functions are being handled automatically as the various activities of the firm are linked by streams of information ("data highways"). In the firms we interviewed there seems to be a trend also toward decentralizing research and development operations to move them closer to the marketing and production functions in the firm.

Firms that are implementing new computer-based manufacturing technologies have found that many of the human decisions that were previously required are now being done automatically. Open loops in production systems are being closed. In these cases, rules are worked out ahead of time that permit the decisions to be automated. Entire processes now move too quickly to allow for human intervention. Similarly, the compression of time between process steps forces those decisions that still require human intervention to be made by the individuals most directly in contact with the production process. In virtually every firm that was experimenting with integrated manufacturing systems we found a keen understanding of the need to push decision-making to lower levels. Not only did we find this concept to be ubiquitous, but we also found this phrasing, "pushing decision-making to lower levels," to be widespread, indicating a recognition that there was some effort involved in getting greater responsibility transferred to the lower ranks. One technologist commented:

> [It used to be that in] introducing a numerically controlled machine or any other type of automation to the [factory] floor, the majority of the people that you [would] affect were the people that actually worked in that environment. Whereas, what we're talking about [now] is actually causing a reorganization of the entire corporate structure and putting a lot of pressure on management to provide these changes and to make a smooth transition for the employees that work for them. The major pressures will be on management.

By pushing operating decisions to lower levels, the corporate-level management and staff is freed to focus on longer-term strategic issues. Computer/telecommunications technology will play a role here, too. Integrated communications and data analysis technology will make it possible for the computer-literate executive to draw off his or her own figures for evaluation of a given situation. This, too, will have an impact on the composition of the workforce in corporate headquarters. Fewer intermediaries will be needed to gather and analyze data and the data can be more timely and accurate.

It appears clear from our interviews that the centralized corporate headquarters is likely to shrink in size, if not in importance, during the coming decade. For large firms, the role played by the headquarters organization will tend to focus on longer-term product strategy and financial, technical, marketing, manufacturing, and human resource planning. Some of the corporate staffs we interviewed were very much aware of mounting criticism that the focus of American top management on short-term performance was contributing to the inability of these firms to compete in international markets. They were in agreement that a shift in policies was necessary.

INTERDEPENDENCE

Shifts toward higher levels of technological complexity seem to be creating situations where firms are moving toward greater dependence on suppliers for certain goods and services. This may, in fact, be a trend away from vertical integration and toward subcontracting as a way of life. In a period of technological change the firm that concentrates on product design and assembly has much greater freedom to shift to sources that provide superior techniques, products, or service. Evidence of this trend came in discussions of software development. Few of the firms that we interviewed are internally creating software for their own automated equipment. The cost of doing so is much higher than the cost of purchasing software from a vendor, even when the software must be modified to fit the firm's equipment. This is a significant change from only a decade ago. The increased competence of software service firms was given as the principal reason for this change.

More subcontracting may also occur for parts and subassemblies. One reason for this may be the pressures of shorter product life-cycles, but it may also be a cost avoidance strategy. One firm candidly told us that they arranged for subcontracts with firms that did not have entrenched labor unions as a means of reducing the high costs associated with in-house production.

Subcontracting also provides increased flexibility to accommodate changes in product design. A firm with large foundries, for example, will find it difficult to consider adopting alternative materials such as plastics, composites, or ceramics for their products because of its sunk investments and its commitments to its workforce.

We found that most of the firms do not have the capability to design their own production equipment. The design capabilities of the firm are generally directed toward product design or toward production process optimization within the context of an existing stock of production machinery, rather than toward designing new production equipment. At least one observer has commented that this may be a key difference between the United States and Japan. Robert Hayes surveyed a number of Japanese manufacturing facilities and was surprised to find that, in general, at least half the production equipment was actually built in-house and that most of the equipment not built internally was at least designed by the firm itself.[26] This seems to be partially related to a desire to have the machines optimized for a particular function within the Japanese factory, but also seems to be due to a realization that a firm's peak demand for machine tools was likely to occur at the same time as for other firms, and as a result, machine tool manufacturers would not be able to provide sufficiently rapid deliveries during periods when all firms were ordering new machines.

SUMMARY

The evidence indicates we are dealing with a phenomenon occurring on an enormously broad front, and the changes implied affect the basic nature of manufacturing firms. We expect that:

☐ Faster throughput time and product change-over time will drastically curtail planning and scheduling time horizons, reduce inventories, and cut batch sizes.

☐ Faster design and design-to-manufacture transition times will result in more rapid product changes, customization, and shorter product life-cycles.

☐ Increases in productive unit size will persist in the continuous process industries, but scale-up is less attractive than increasing flexibility in discrete manufacturing.

☐ Plant size will tend to be governed by factors other than the direct effect of new technology: transportation, resource availability, organizational effectiveness, and supplier relationships.

☐ Restructuring of organizations in the manufacturing firm will tend to push operating decisions to lower levels, eliminate data gatherers and analysts, and emphasize longer-term perspectives for top management.

☐ The firm of the future will depend more heavily on outside suppliers for software, materials, parts and subassemblies, and production machines.

The emerging picture is that of a leaner, somewhat more specialized firm, more flexible in manufacturing processes and market response, with operating decisions being made on a decentralized basis. None of this provides any indication that a manufacturing manager's job is going to be any easier in the future. On the contrary, it is likely to become substantially more challenging and exciting. This will become even more evident when we examine human resource impacts in the next chapter.

5

IMPLICATIONS OF EVOLVING TECHNOLOGY

The Workforce

Every time significant changes in manufacturing technology have occurred in this country there has been an impact on (1) the number of people required for a given level of output, (2) the skills of people involved with the new technology, and (3) the relationships among members of the workforce. We can be sure that computer/telecommunications technologies will also trigger important consequences in each of these three areas.

If we are trying to predict the nature of the changes that will take place this time, we must be alert to the fact that these changes are occurring in an ongoing social, economic, and political environment. Conditions in a given environment will influence not only what happens, but also the magnitude and rate of the effect. If economic conditions are such, for example, that there is a substantial and chronic labor surplus, the productivity increases that result from these new processes can have much more adverse consequences for the workforce than if the economy is growing and there is minimal unemployment.

The realities in our current world include the fact that the competitive position of American manufacturing firms in both domestic and international markets has weakened. American producers can no longer count on the superiority of their goods in quality, variety, novelty, style, or cost. Competition from products of other countries in all of these categories places the American producer in the position of having to try to excel in many dimensions at the same time. This task is made more difficult by another reality—the same or similar manufacturing technologies are readily available to producers in other industrial countries. America is no longer the technologically dominant country it was 30 years ago. Other countries have learned to adopt advanced technology quickly and effectively. They have frequently taken the lead in innovative process development. This change makes the speed with which new technology is adopted by American firms a crucially important issue.

A further reality is that we have accumulated a national heritage of traditions, attitudes, practices, agreements, laws, and regulations that influence or constrain the directions in which changes can proceed. Past events have woven a web within which we live. While part of what has occurred provides a framework of strength and protection for present endeavors, much of our legacy is an impediment to technological progress. This latter aspect is so important to the consideration of technology strategy that it receives separate attention in Chapter 6.

Unless these factors are recognized, no attempt to identify human impacts can have much meaning, and subsequent efforts to define policy alternatives to ameliorate adverse consequences will be of little value. Our discussion proceeds within the context of these realities.

LABOR DISPLACEMENT

There is no question that, where computer-based automation replaces conventional processes, it reduces the number of workers needed per unit of output. If production volumes do not increase correspondingly, labor displacement will occur. We use the term *displacement* advisedly here, and we define displacement broadly, so it includes forced changes of type of job, job location, or work group within the same firm as well as changes to another firm or changes involving unemployment.

The field interviews connected with this study, plus earlier case studies of installations of advanced technology, provide some insight into the magnitude of displacement that can be directly associated with the technology. These studies cannot, however, inform us about whether the changes mean increased or decreased employment in the economy. The level of unemployment depends so much on other factors, such as general economic conditions, population changes, foreign competition, and governmental fiscal and monetary policies, all of which can either compensate for or exacerbate unemployment caused by technological displacement. By automating its process in a favorable economic climate, for example, a firm may so improve its competitive position that demand for its products here and abroad far exceeds the capacity of its workforce even with the productivity increases. Added employment may be the result. Another firm may find itself forced to adopt new technology as a purely defensive measure against strong foreign competition, merely to retain its market share. Its move may very likely increase unemployment, at least temporarily. In both instances, however, a substantial amount of displacement will have occurred as employees shift from one job to another, one location to another, or one company to another. As we have defined it, displacement *may* involve temporary or even permanent unemployment, but it is not equivalent to unemployment.

The important issues from this perspective are the transitional effects that impact individuals, not the long-run macroeconomic effects that are measured by national statistics. Displacements are transitional events. They are important not only because they affect employment levels but also because their various forms directly influence employee attitudes, particularly those attitudes toward acceptance of future changes. Receptivity of the workforce to technological change can be regarded as the summation of gains and losses experienced and anticipated by every member of the workforce. The worker who is about to lose a valued personal relationship within a particular work group because of a robot installation will resist the change unless there are perceived gains that outweigh the loss. Expressed by employees in many different ways, resistance slows down or stops changes, adds costs, and distorts results. We consider this aspect of technological change in greater detail in the next chapter, and we summarize here our findings on the magnitude of the displacements involved.

In our interviews, firms that had recently introduced more highly automated or integrated production facilities were specifically asked to discuss changes in the number of production employees directly attributable to the introduction of new production processes. Table 1 summarizes the responses we received. In many cases, labor requirements for a particular production unit did not decrease, but output increased, permitting the use of fewer production units for a given level of output. For comparison purposes, the figures in this table are normalized to a constant output level, so that a firm that doubled output with the same number of employees is re-

TABLE 1. Percentage Decrease in Labor Requirements in Typical New Production Processes

Firm	Process/Discrete Manufacturing	Percentage Decrease in Labor Content
A	Process	35 to 65
B	Process	40 to 90
C	Process	85
D	Process	80
E	Discrete	30 to 40
F	Discrete	70

ported as having a 50 percent decline in labor content just as is a firm that halves its labor force with a constant level of output.

At first blush these numbers appear to be astonishingly high. A single generation improvement in manufacturing technology may result in eliminating more than three-quarters of the production labor that had previously been required. Furthermore, these are not estimated labor savings due to technologies that firms were contemplating. These are estimates based on reports of actual operating experience. In our interviews we heard manufacturing managers talk about processes that had been implemented that resulted in manufacturing employment falling dramatically. In one case a plant that years ago required 15,000 employees is now being operated with 2000. In another case a new set of machines had been installed that resulted in nine times the output of the machines they replaced and required only the same number of employees. Another firm experienced a quadrupling of output while reducing labor by 20 percent.

In one early installation of a major flexible manufacturing system, six computer-controlled machining centers were linked together by an automated conveyor system. Each center had automatic tool changing and automatic workpiece locating capabilities. The six-machine system was tended by a crew of three or four operators, depending on the shift, and these operators handled all of the tasks of loading, unloading, tool replacement, minor maintenance, inspection, and system monitoring. The system had the equivalent capacity of 33 individual machine tools, which would have required a workforce about 10 times the actual crew size.

These figures were provided by knowledgeable individuals within the firms, and they give some indication of the degree to which the incorporation of computer-based manufacturing processes can result in a revolutionary change in the labor content of output. The numbers cannot be used, however, to express short-term (1- to 3-year) consequences for the general employment level in a firm. The introduction of new technology clearly can have an immense impact on the labor requirements of a particular production process within a single plant, but its effect on the labor requirements of the firm as a whole will be diminished for two reasons. First, the introduction of new technology within firms is an evolutionary process that occurs quite slowly. Most of the firms that we interviewed had only one or perhaps two facilities where computer-integrated manufacturing technologies had been introduced on a scale sufficient to have a dramatic impact on the amount of production labor required. Each of these firms had long-range plans to spread these technologies throughout the firm, either by retrofitting existing facilities, or, as was more often the case, by building new plants and closing existing ones. Each step of this kind, however, represents a 3- to 5-year project, and the steps are being taken in piecemeal fashion.

There was a substantial range of views, even within firms, concerning the period of time required to complete the conversion process to computer-integrated manufacturing. In at least two firms we found a prevalent view that their manufacturing facilities would look pretty much the same in 10 years as they do today. This was attributed to forecasts of relatively slow growth or even decline in customer demand, and to existing overcapacity in the industry. Individuals in other firms held the view that in 10 years virtually all of their plants would be using production processes at least as efficient as the computer-integrated systems presently available. Opinions often diverged, even within a single firm. In one company, when a group of upper-level managers was asked what proportion of their production facilities would be updated within 10 years to the level they had achieved in a sophisticated new plant just completed, the estimates ranged from 50 to 90 percent.

A second reason that the estimates in Table 1 overstate the quantity of labor displacement in firms in general is that they refer only to the number of production workers directly engaged in the processes affected by the change. They are not a measure of the percentage of the total plant population or of the corporation as a whole. Although it is clear that computer/ telecommunications technology will significantly increase productivity in nonproduction functions of the firm also, it seems unlikely that the labor savings will be as large as those in Table 1. One electronics company vice-president expressed the view that in the future, manufacturing itself would become a relatively smaller part of the functions of the firm as a whole, and that functions such as research, product development, and marketing would assume greater relative importance.

The first of these two qualifications merely provides insight into the timing of the changes. It does not reduce the long-term impact. So, when we add in productivity gains from computer-aided design, office automation, and expert systems, the only sensible conclusion is that *substantially* fewer people will be required in the future to produce any given amount of goods. A number of the companies in our study have this understanding. One firm, for example, estimated that one-third of its total employees would not be needed within 10 years.

In many of the firms the transition to computer-based manufacturing is already well under way. Displacement effects, however, have tended to be masked by the effects of the recession that began in 1981. A number of individuals confided to us that it was common knowledge that the recession had been used as a tool for making labor force cutbacks that ultimately would have been required anyway. These changes did not simply involve union "give-backs" or work rule alterations, but also involved paring down the workforce to a size appropriate for the kind of production processes that would be more common in a post-recession economy.

Groups of people other than production workers will also experience displacement in manufacturing firms because of the new technologies. It is likely that there will be fewer factory supervisors and foremen. Improved data acquisition and communications technologies will make it possible for supervisors to oversee larger production units, so the level of product output per supervisor will increase, while the number of people supervised decreases.

Manufacturing support people—production schedulers, inventory controllers, expeditors, quality control clerks, dispatchers, and the like—will be affected by the integration of processing functions and the automation of decisions concerning schedules, quality, movement of materials, and product output. The telescoping of time between operations and the ability of the computer to handle lower-level decisions will remove the need for large specialized staff functions. This will apply to both professionals and nonprofessionals in these areas.

A similar reduction will be seen in the staffs of "transactions processors" or data gatherers and analyzers, both at the factory level and at higher levels of the corporate structure. When corporate executives become skilled in the use of computer interfaces, their need to have staffs to gather and predigest information will be greatly reduced, and corporate headquarters will become leaner and less bureaucratic.

SKILLS

Technological change will not only have a quantitative effect on manufacturing jobs, but there will also be a qualitative effect in terms of job skills. Two kinds of skills impacts need to be considered. First, there are changes in the *nature* of the skills that will be called for, regardless of whether these skills are higher or lower on the pay scale of the firm. How does the nature of a person's job change when he or she must interact with production systems where both machines and materials are controlled by computers that also communicate with other machines, with staff support people, and, perhaps, even with the person's boss?

The second kind of change is in the *distribution* of skills levels. In this case we are concerned about changes in the relative numbers of jobs at various levels in the organization and whether the changes in this distribution will affect personal growth, advancement, or upward mobility. We will look at these two subjects separately, but will keep in mind that they are closely related to each other and to other issue areas.

The list of factory worker skills required by the new computer/telecommunications technology includes at least the following:

1. Visualization—the ability to manipulate mental patterns.

2. Conceptual thinking (or abstract reasoning).

3. Understanding of process phenomena—machine functions and machine/material interactions.

4. Statistical inference—appreciation of trends, limits, meaning of data.

5. Verbal communication, oral and visual.

6.   Attentiveness.

7.   Individual responsibility.

These skills are not listed in any order of importance. In fact, we have found in case studies that the last in the list appears to be a very significant criterion for selecting people to run new computer-controlled machine installations. An ability and willingness to take individual responsibility for a portion of the production process and for the products passing through it becomes increasingly important as the number of jobs in the operation declines. In one instance of advanced automation, the need to be able to select people who exhibited "responsible behavior" was cited as the reason for increasing the pay rate of the job even though other skills requirements were reduced.

We can use the process industries to some extent for models of how skills changes are likely to proceed, since these industries (chemicals, petrochemicals, paper, utilities) have already experienced many of the changes now occurring more broadly. For those industries, computerization and closed-loop automation began in the 1950s and now is a mature technology. Jobs in these industries have also matured (or have disappeared). The jobs that are left exhibit characteristics that are quite similar to descriptions of new forms of work expected for today's computer-based technologies.

The direction of manufacturing skills changes is from physically involved, manipulative, tactile, "hands on" type of work to that which is conceptual, cognitive, and based on an abstract understanding of the process. Instead of maintaining close physical contact with the product and with the process through touch, sight, sound, and smell, the production worker stands aside while the integrated combination of computers and machines proceeds with minimal direct human intervention. In one job of this kind a worker loads a workpiece into a computer-controlled machining center and starts the machine. For the next 7 1/2 hours, while the machine makes the myriad cuts required, the worker merely attends the machine, intervening only once, about 4 hours into the process, to reorient the part in its fixture. In this particular instance, the worker remains at the machine, attentive to the way the machine is performing. The workpiece is large and valuable, as is the machine. A broken tool, a loose fixture, a defect in the workpiece, or a "glitch" in a computer program could cause thousands of dollars of damage in a few seconds. The worker is *monitoring* the process rather than being a part of it.

The removal of the worker from physical contact may go so far as to transfer the workplace from the machine area into a control room remote from the process. At this point virtually all direct sensory perception of process conditions is eliminated and the worker must rely on computer-furnished information for his or her knowledge of what is happening. In some instances, such as in nuclear power plants, remote monitoring is the only feasible approach. In other situations, where there is excessive noise or fumes in the production area, it is highly desirable. In a large number of cases, however, it is a means of providing collective monitoring of a number of process stages with just a few operators. It also keeps people from directly tinkering with the process. Making the switch-over to closed loop control of one sophisticated new paper machine, for example, was only accomplished after the workers on the floor were persuaded to operate from the control room and stop making manual adjustments that confused the computer.

The characteristics of new production jobs, then, will tend to include monitoring of the process, possibly remotely, but at least removed from direct physical involvement. This tendency will show up in all stages of manufacture from primary processes through fabrication and into assembly and test. The more reliable the process and the more trustworthy the sensors, the more remote the workers are likely to be.

It may be argued that this description does not apply to maintenance workers, setup mechanics, and similar skilled tradespeople. Even here, however, the computer - machine connection becomes so intimate that diagnostics of trouble and prescribed remedies can be provided by the computer at great distances. Some major machinery manufacturers now offer computer-based diagnostic services where the computer controlling the production machine is linked by telephone to a diagnostic computer hundreds of miles away.

A similar situation occurs for other forms of manufacturing jobs. Those responsible for scheduling, keeping count of output, evaluating quality, collecting costs, or monitoring efficiency are all becoming dependent on the computer to provide the information, to perform analyses, and to report results. Instead of sending an expeditor to locate a job and move it on through the shop, the production control coordinator interrogates a cathode ray tube and, if a change in priority is appropriate, inserts this into the computer's working instructions and a new schedule is accomplished.

Nearly everyone we spoke with told us that the new jobs would require greater technical skill. Upon closer examination, however, we found that the term *technical skill* was being used to describe a familiarity and ability to feel "comfortable" with technical processes, principally computers. It was felt that people will be needed who are not intimidated by computer terminal CRT displays and who are able to interact with these displays to obtain required information and issue appropriate commands. It is deceptive to label such skill as highly technical. The situation is much like that of driving a car. One does not have to know the theory of internal combustion engines or how the power gets to the wheels in order to get around in traffic. Similarly, workers connected with computer-managed processes will generally not be required to know very much about how computers work. They will have no need to learn conventional programming or anything in particular about digital circuits. They may have to learn, however, how to use specific user-friendly software packages, how to adapt to changes in software, the capabilities and limitations of the different kinds of data storage media, and where information comes from and where it goes.

Manufacturing managers in plants where computer-integrated manufacturing technologies have been introduced tell us that, in general, they have had little or no trouble bringing people up to this level of computer familiarity relatively quickly. This may be due in part, however, to the fact that frequently in early installations only the more adaptable employees have been selected for the work. It is a bit too early to tell whether all employees will be able to adapt to computer-integrated processes with little or no difficulty.

A few firms reported that older workers' responses were significantly different from those of younger workers. While all workers were able to respond appropriately to cues for action given by the computer through the CRT, younger employees generally went further, asking the computer to provide data on the production process and "playing" with the system almost as if it were a toy, in order to find ways to optimize the production process. Older employees were less able to attain this second level of familiarity. Perhaps one reason for this is the early exposure that younger workers have received to CRT devices that include two-way communication. One technologist commented:

> I argue with some people in terms of the importance of the video game craze that we're in now. A lot of people are against it. My way of thinking is that it's part of this training. You get comfortable with sitting there playing the video game and it's

not that much unlike sitting there having your production line going on out there and you're monitoring things on the tube. . . . You're dealing with the black box. . . . The kind of people that will be willing to do that kind of job are probably being trained in our video arcades today.

One interesting aspect of the development of computer-based technology is that the more sophisticated the application, the less visible the computer becomes. Microprocessors are being "buried" in the machines themselves, controlling major functions without any interaction of any sort with the operator. "Smart" sensors, combining both a sensing element and a microcomputer, are not only able to detect deviations from normal, but can figure out what to do about them. Routine adjustments of this kind are handled without the operator's knowledge. The implication of this trend is that even the rather limited computer interaction skills currently needed will tend to disappear with time.

Remote process monitoring and control, however, can involve two challenging new skills: *visualizing* the process and its condition from information presented, and *conceptualizing* or reasoning what actions if any are needed to keep the system running properly.

As computer-integrated systems proliferate and expand in scope, it will become more and more important for workers to understand how the entire production process fits together, rather than simply working with a small piece of it. In the past, mechanization of a process resulted in production work being broken up into a series of relatively simple tasks. Each worker was then responsible for only his or her piece of the production process. Often employees had no idea how the rest of the system outside of their own area actually functioned. As the sequence of operations now becomes more highly integrated under computer management, this extreme division of work will no longer be possible. Each operator will be responsible for several stages in the process and for knowing how his or her part of the system connects with what precedes or follows it.

Attempts by companies to produce higher quality, more consistent products will be facilitated by more versatile sensing devices and by the number crunching ability of the computer. Workers will need to know what the numbers mean and what action, if any, is required of them. Firms in this country have rarely attempted to teach workers any aspects of statistics or statistical inference. Now, however, this will become a routine part of the job for many who are monitoring machine performance or operating inspection systems. Because few schools teach statistics prior to college level instruction, the present workforce generally is lacking in this skill.

The ability to communicate has not normally been one of the criteria for blue collar worker selection. As long as the worker has been able to follow instructions and seek help when it is needed, he or she has not been required to possess any unusual abilities to communicate with fellow workers, with supervisors, or with the production process. This situation changes when a machine monitor's job includes giving clear, unambiguous instruction to the system or providing information to downstream workers or to supervisors on the state of the production process. Equally important will be the ability to receive and understand messages from co-workers or from computer interfaces.

When production operations can continue for hours without human intervention and the only requirement for a human overseer is to determine that the machines are functioning properly, the ability to keep alert and attentive to possible system failures becomes a key job characteristic. It is the kind of task that many people have difficulty doing for long periods of time. As systems become so reliable that the probability of failure becomes very low (one event out of a thousand or 10 thousand), the human system tends not to be a reliable monitor. This is the problem experienced in nuclear power stations, where nothing is supposed to go wrong, but the possible consequences of a failure make it necessary to demand high levels of attentiveness from the operating crew. While the consequences of machine failure in manufacturing are in no way commensurate with those of a nuclear power plant, they can be so costly that this requirement has high implicit value even when it is not spelled out in hiring or advancement criteria.

Production jobs that may be isolated both from the machines and from other workers as well require a strong individual sense of responsiblity. We have evidence that operating managers are recognizing this fact, even to the extent of bending conventional personnel policies to select the "right" people for key jobs. This situation was described in an unpublished case study of the application of advanced automation technology in a major industrial firm:

> Comparisons between machine operators' jobs on conventional stand-alone machines and those on the automated machining systems demonstrated substantial changes in the nature of the jobs. Despite the fact that the workpieces and the machining operations performed were technically almost identical in nature to that which had been performed in the building for years, the change in the nature of the machines toward much higher levels of automation significantly altered the job content and skills requirements of the operators. The older jobs on conventional machines had a high degree of autonomy, discretion, freedom of movement, responsibility, group interaction and control. The new jobs on the automated machines required, in contrast, the performance of prescribed functions involving limited judgement, some conceptual skills and abstract reasoning, carried out over long periods of monitoring vigilance in isolation. The key job characteristic in the

eyes of management was "responsible behavior" that safe-
guarded the investment in the machines and the product.
Relative to the comparable older jobs, these newer jobs had
less autonomy and control.[27]

In this particular instance, the jobs on the automated machines were given higher ratings than those for conventional
machines where the normal skills requirements were higher.
This enabled management to select the people they wanted
for the new jobs rather than being forced to accept people
according to seniority rules.

The second issue with respect to skills is the *distribution* of
skills requirements. Will the computer/communications technology call for more high-skilled jobs or will there be a de-
skilling of the labor force? As was mentioned earlier, certain
occupational groups become targets for technological displacement. What will be the cumulative effect on the manufacturing organization?

This is an important subject for almost everyone in manufacturing, because decisions made about the skill levels of jobs
will have a major bearing on career paths, opportunities for
advancement, modes of acquiring skills, income, and job
satisfaction.

The level of skill required to do a job can be determined only
after the job itself is defined. Jobs usually consist of a group of
elements or tasks. Because there is a considerable amount of
latitude in the way a job can be put together, the distribution
of needed skills within a given workforce can be a matter of
management policy. We have indicated that there will be
changes in the *character* of the skills demanded by advanced
technology, but the *level* of skills required for any given job,
whether high or low, will depend on which elements of the
work are combined to make up the job. An inspector's job, for
example, may simply involve checking curcuits for missing or

poorly made connections using equipment that is set up and programmed by others. The job might also, however, involve checking other components, reworking faulty pieces, and programming or reprogramming the computer-controlled inspection machine for different batches of parts.

This discretionary aspect in the creation of jobs should be kept in mind throughout the discussion of skills distribution. Jobs can be put together in many different ways. What we describe is what is likely to take place if current tendencies persist. These effects are not mandated by the technology, however. Computer-based technology affords exceptionally great latitude in job design. Under the right conditions, the distribution of job skills in a plant can be tailored to match a desired goal.

Traditional engineering design philosophies, however, tend to encourage process designs in which jobs require less and less skill. Engineers will change their design philosophies only if guided by changed management policies and attitudes. Firms that are unaware of the skills issue are unlikely to make the necessary policy changes. Many other firms that are aware of the skills issue may be unwilling to change their policies, because they see an opportunity to weaken the political or economic power of the workforce. The future strength of American manufacturing, however, will be determined largely by those firms who deliberately set out to design solutions to human issues while they are designing ways to use the new technology. More will be said about the policy alternatives in job design in a later chapter.

If past practices in job definition prevail, then new manufacturing technology will have a substantial impact on skill profiles of factory workers. In most large conventional manufacturing plants we find that there is a reasonably broad spectrum of jobs ranging from the very lowest, "entry-level" jobs to those requiring a high degree of skill or proficiency.

This spectrum or distribution of jobs tends to be continuous, that is, for any given job level in the spectrum there are likely to be jobs of slightly higher levels of skills to which one might expect to advance. If we plot the distribution of jobs for plants of this type, the curve might look something like Figure 4. The shape of the curve might differ, depending on the nature of the work to be done in a given plant. Plants with a large amount of light assembly work might see the bulge in distribution nearer the low end of the scale; those with a great deal of precision machining and testing might find the bulge somewhat higher.

What happens to this curve when computer/telecommunications technology becomes prevalent? As we indicated earlier in this chapter, displacement will cause the curve to shrink toward the baseline as the overall number of people needed for a given level of output is reduced. Displacement, however, is not likely to affect all levels in the plant in the same way, and this is where some forms of computer-based automation may produce serious difficulties.

The kinds of jobs that are most difficult to automate, even with computer assistance, are those that require a high degree of geographic mobility, continuous use of visual and tactile sensing, use of a multiplicity of tools in nonrepetitive tasks, and problem solving in unpredictable, poorly defined situations. It is interesting that such jobs can be found both at the very lowest levels and at the highest levels of the spectrum. Maintenance workers and engineers may not feel flattered that their jobs share the same characteristics as sweepers and custodians, but both groups can be comforted that they are less likely to be displaced by a computer-controlled machine.

The jobs that can be automated are those in a relatively fixed location, those where the process has determinate and easily sensed parameters, and those that call for a relatively limited repertoire of activities. These jobs, which are the cur-

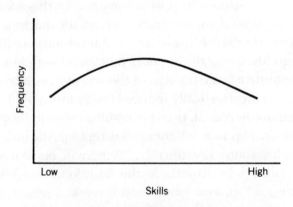

FIGURE 4
Distribution of Skills in Conventional Plant

rent targets for automation, are the machine operating and assembly jobs. Machine operating jobs include such classifications as lathe operator, press operator, welder, painter, plater, or inspector. Assembly jobs have traditionally been difficult to automate because of the need for both visual and tactile sensing, qualities possessed by most humans but difficult to give to robots. Recent advances in sensing techniques, in accessory fixtures to aid workpiece positioning, and in product design for ease of assembly have made automated assembly much more feasible, however, and we can expect to see increasing applications of automation in this area.

What happens if we automate, say, all the machine operator jobs in the plant? These are mid-level jobs, requiring a fairly high level of skill. In many metalworking plants these jobs constitute a large fraction of the workforce. If these jobs disappear or are drastically reduced (by factors of 7:1 to 10:1 as discussed in Chapter 2), then the resulting distribution of jobs may look like Figure 5, where a valley replaces the bulge in the skills distribution. Presumably, there will be a few more highly skilled jobs to handle the additional machine programming, setup, and maintenance work. Perhaps the few remaining machine operators who are monitoring machine systems will be adjudged to require higher skills, but this is somewhat questionable. Unless given programming, maintenance, quality control, or other responsibilities it is likely that monitoring of machine sytems will eventually be considered to have lower skill requirements (or the monitoring itself will be automated).

Distributions of skills of this kind are not imaginary. A recent case study of an electric utility company revealed that computer-based automation had completely removed all mid-range operating jobs in the generating plant, leaving only low-level unskilled jobs and second and first class engineers.

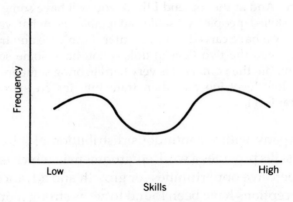

FIGURE 5
Possible Distribution in Computer-based Automation

The company was experiencing difficulty in finding qualified people for the second class engineering positions.[28]

When asked about future skill requirements, a technologist at one of the firms said:

> Generally, the way the workforce is designed, or happens to be, you have a spectrum with a lot of people at the lower end—manual work—and then you tail down to the top end, where you have very highly skilled technicians. You have people in a band throughout. When you turn totally towards more robotics applications, I think you will have the lower skills, but all these people at the center will vanish, they won't be there. And at the top end I think you will have some very highly skilled people, versatile, adaptable. So what you've done is you have carved out the center. I can't see any transition between the two (levels) unless you have some sort of program. But the point is, it is very hard to bring someone into a very low level job and then train him for an extremely technical level. . . .

A company with a continuous distribution of jobs over a range of skills provides a work environment in which employees can perceive opportunities for growth and advancement. Such perceptions have been found to act as strong motivators for human performance. In talking with technical and manufacturing managers we explored the hypothesis that the elimination of medium-skilled jobs would make advancement for unskilled employees difficult. We found that few managers had given much thought to the issue of career paths available within their firms. Apparently, many firms do not have formal career counseling services for their employees, even though they may support continuing education for them in one form or another. Those managers who expressed a view for the most part felt that high-skilled labor was most often obtained outside the firm and that there were few, if any, instances of individuals advancing from low-skill to high-skill jobs within the firm. One company did have a test that low-skilled workers could take to qualify for higher-skilled jobs, but it was reputed to be impossibly difficult, serving more as a barrier to advancement than as a conduit.

In addition to assessing general skill levels, firms were asked to identify the job categories that would require more people in coming years. By far, the most often mentioned high-growth jobs were in software design. Several firms mentioned software design as the most critical bottleneck to the implementation of computer-integrated manufacturing technology. A number of people also expressed the view, however, that in the near future software would be available that would itself write software. One individual suggested that this had to be the case because there simply would not be enough capable humans available to do this job.

Firms also identified engineers, particularly electrical engineers, as likely to be in greater demand. As product life-cycles shorten, the engineering-intensive functions of research, product development, and production start-up will receive greater emphasis. Engineers will also be called on for the design, selection and implementation of the new computer/telecommunications technologies.

In some cases it is easier to predict what type of work will need to be performed in the future than to say what category of individual will perform it. We know, for example, that there will be a critical need for individuals who can conceive of manufacturing as a whole and design integrated production facilities. The individuals who design these integrated systems may be called software engineers, systems analysts, system architecture specialists, or manufacturing engineers. Other titles may be invented. These individuals will be required to design systems of data flows and the mechanisms through which the data will interface with the various parts of the production process. This will involve a technical understanding of production processes as well as a grasp of the marketing, inventory, and accounting aspects of the firm. Psychology and physiology will come into play to ensure that the designs are comfortable to humans and manageable. They will also need to understand the politics of various institutional structures within the firm. Design of sophisticated software may require groups having a range of backgrounds. An individual's ability to integrate these factors, however, is likely to be prized above all others in tomorrow's firms.

Our observations on the effect of computer/communications technology on workforce skills, then, is that the nature of skills called for will change, but how these skills are distributed among those in the workforce will depend on decisions made by individual firms in structuring their jobs. If current practices continue, there is a danger that serious gaps or bottlenecks in job progression may occur, setting up conditions that can cause frustration and alienation among lower levels of job holders.

RELATIONSHIPS

As the nature of work changes, relationships among members of the workforce will also change. It appears, for instance, that social distance will tend to increase, a result of greater physical isolation of workers from each other and increased dependence on computer interfaces for information. There is a chance that increased mobility afforded workers by computer controls will give them opportunities to continue social contacts, but this does not appear to have been the case in many of the situations we have observed. Relationships with supervisors will also change. As a supervisor's span of responsibility for production operations increases and his or her span of responsibility for numbers of workers declines, each worker's role becomes more important, and each worker must take on a certain amount of autonomy.

In large measure, production employees will oversee themselves. They will be expected to assess problems as they develop, to determine whether assistance is needed from others, and to summon assistance from the appropriate people. There will simply be no time to refer most problems to foremen or managers for resolution. Increased judgment will be required as decision-making is pushed to lower levels. Production employees will also assume an ever greater responsibility for quality control within the firm. In short, employees will be expected to behave responsibly, to understand the goals of the firm, and to act without direct supervision to implement those goals in the production process. The implication is that the worker will become *individualized*, not lost in a mass of people having identical jobs, identical titles, and minimal recognition. Regardless of skill level or pay level, the worker of the future will be disconnected from the machine and from the comfortable anonymity of the group. This can be frightening or rewarding, depending on how each individual situation is handled.

The role of managers will change dramatically as well. A high degree of delegation of authority will be required. A reduced and restructured labor force may also mean that many managers who previously had supervisory responsibilities over a large number of workers will now oversee substantially smaller staffs. Members of these staffs will come to expect a collegial relationship, rather than a chain of command. Furthermore, managers may find that the type of work they do is not very different from the work done by those who are technically "below" them. As a result, managers who have in the past defined their worth in terms of the number of people under them or in terms of their ability to exercise authority may have a very difficult time adjusting to the new manufacturing environment. One technologist that we interviewed, for example, believed that the barrier to technology adoption was managerial resistance:

> The real problem is not going to be with the mechanic on the floor. . . . What's really going to cause us the problem is middle and upper-middle management. That's where the real problem is. The reason being that as you become a first level manager and a second level manager and ultimately a third level manager, it is a direct function of the number of people under your control. . . . The problem is . . . that the truth [about productivity gains] is not getting out because the managers want to hang on to their people.

The new relationship between employees and the firm will require a significantly greater degree of mutual trust than has been evidenced in the past. The decisions that employees are expected to make could cost the firm substantial sums of money, but firms that do not trust employees could incur even more substantial penalties. They may find themselves unable to exploit new technology, or they may have to pay engineers or supervisors to do the work that could be handled at subordinate levels.

If factory workers are to be given greater decision-making responsibility, however, they must be willing to part with work rules that constrain the range of work an individual can do. Job jurisdiction rules, for instance, that confine a person's activities to tasks of only one kind are not consonant with increased discretionary authority. Willingness to give up work rules means that employees must trust their employers. Many of these rules were established at the insistence of employees to protect themselves from abuse. A relationship of trust is a reciprocal relationship. Firms in which employees refuse to place greater trust in their managements will have many of the same difficulties experienced by firms where the distrust originates among its management.

Given a history of conflict resolution through confrontation rather than cooperation, it is unclear whether American labor unions and management will be able to meet the challenge posed by advanced technologies. To avoid the confrontation, many companies have consciously sought to locate new automated plants in places where there would be no unions. Executives of one firm confided to us that this factor was a critical one in plant location decisions and that plant managers in such locations had been fired for not being able to block the entrance of a union. We must ask the question whether the only two alternatives available to labor and management in the 1990s must be either the confrontation policies of past decades or a total lack of collective bargaining representation for workers. Down the confrontation path lies a form of paralysis that will stifle adoption of new technology. Down the nonunion path lies the danger of inequitable sharing of the fruits of the new technology and lack of protection of workers from capricious management decisions.

The impact of today's automation on the labor force will be substantially different from that which has been observed over the past 100 years of industrialization. In the past, automation was designed to reduce processes to relatively simple tasks. For low-skilled employees, work became extremely routine, mind-numbing, and, at times, dehumanizing. The current wave of automation is eliminating many of these mindless tasks. The most boring, most dangerous, and least desirable jobs are the first candidates for automation. New automation can bring employees into the decision-making process, giving them new responsibilities and challenges. It can put a premium on conceptual, creative thinking, and on individual performance and responsibility. Old attitudes between managers and workers may require major change.

Where these changes do occur there can be some remarkable results. In one plant where computer control has been introduced into a continuous-process manufacturing environment, operators have been given a major role in controlling the process. It was reported that many of the plant operators were staying after work to play with the capabilities of the computerized process simulator. One of the problems for this firm was in getting its employees to go home.

6

THE AVAILABILITY OF TOMORROW'S WORKFORCE

Forecasting the total supply of workers over a 10-year time frame is a relatively simple matter, involving principally an assessment of demographic trends and labor force participation rates. The assessment becomes considerably more difficult, however, when its goal is to forecast the number of individuals in any particular profession or skill group. This is because the supply of labor in specific skill groups is dependent upon individual career choice decisions, a process that is not well understood by economists, by sociologists, or by psychologists. Labor availability forecasts that are based on the fields of study of individuals while in school or on first job experience are likely to be quite unreliable. Students may elect to take jobs that cannot be predicted by their fields of study, and a person in a first job may opt out of that field of work after a short period of real experience. Only in career areas where formal training is lengthy (medicine, law, specific fields of science) are forecasts likely to be reasonably accurate.

A number of formal and informal forecasts of the future supply/demand balance for labor of specific skill types have been issued by the Department of Labor, the National Science Foundation, various professional groups, and others. The conclusions of these studies are generally couched in terms of a labor market balance, shortage, or surplus. However, studies of this type are generally deficient because they do not explicitly define the terms *balance, shortage,* and *surplus.* With some substantial adjustment lags, labor markets function in a manner similar to other markets: when demand exceeds supply, wages are bid up; when supply exceeds demand, wages tend to fall. In the absence of the adjustment lags, shortages and surpluses could not exist. If the number of workers in any given profession were to fall short of the

number of jobs available, salaries would rise until more workers decided to move into the "shortage" field. In addition, as
wages rise, employers might prefer to do without additional
workers in the "shortage" area. They might choose to retrain
employees working in closely related fields, they might alter
their processes to use different kinds of workers, they might
introduce more productive technology, or they might scale
down production plans.

Labor shortages and surpluses do exist, for two reasons.
Changes in wage rates are slow to reflect the mismatch between job openings and available workers. Even when rates
change, the supply of workers responds slowly to the change.
Several factors cause this wage "rigidity" or "stickiness." It
takes some time for workers and employers to realize that
market conditions have changed. If unemployed workers
have trouble finding jobs, they may initially believe that they
simply have not looked hard enough. If employers have trouble locating additional employees, they may believe that there
is simply a temporary disruption in the market which will be
corrected in the next hiring cycle. Furthermore, even after
employers and workers realize that market conditions have
changed, other factors may prevent them from immediately
making wage adjustments. When labor surpluses occur, factors delaying wage adjustment include long-term labor contracts, wage legislation, and the general tendency of unions to
prefer layoffs over wage rate reductions. When these factors
combine, decreases in real wages are likely to happen very
slowly, through wage increases that are less than the rate of
inflation. Additional delays arise because workers cannot
switch careers instantaneously; often substantial retraining is
required.

For these reasons, labor shortage and surplus figures are
not perfect measures of the magnitude of labor market imbalances. At any given time the apparent size of an imbalance

may reflect more the degree of stickiness of wages than under-lying rates of change in the demand for labor. We urge caution in interpreting shortage and surplus projections, and urge use of the data only as a general indication of labor market conditions.

The introduction of new technology has often created a demand for greater numbers of individuals with particular skills. The advent of the electronic age in manufacturing, for example, has produced a significant demand for electronic technicians. They have been in chronically short supply. In such instances, if the rate of increase in demand for labor skills that are critical to the adoption of new technology runs suffi-ciently far ahead of the rate of increase of supply, real wages will rise. This may put a damper on the rate of adoption of new technology and jeopardize a company's ability to com-pete. From the firm's perspective, then, the question is not whether shortages will exist, but rather whether it will be possible to secure appropriately skilled workers at wage rates that permit it to remain competitive.

The issue of labor availability does depend on changing industrial demands for workers in various skill groups, but public and private strategies can also affect labor availability over the next decade. Job information, training, and place-ment services, for example, can speed labor skills adjust-ments. Retraining programs, in particular, can help fill gaps in skilled labor categories that would otherwise result in ap-parent shortages. Much of retraining, however, is proposed principally to relieve labor surpluses. At present, relatively little attention focuses on whether there will, in fact, be jobs requiring the skills in which surplus workers are being re-trained.

Publicly supported incentive programs to encourage peo-ple to enter certain professions also serve to modify the sup-ply of certain labor skills. There are programs, for example, to increase the number of engineering graduates. Fellowships are given to engineering students and teachers, work/study programs are publicly supported, and direct grants are given to engineering schools. The prospective balance or imbalance in engineering labor markets depends critically on the level of funding of these types of programs.

Public activities also compete with private industry for available labor skills. Rapid increases in defense spending, for example, can have a significant impact on the availability of electrical and aeronautical engineers for the private, non-defense economy. Similarly, a rapidly escalating public program of highway construction, airport expansion, or other infrastructure improvements can impact the availability of civil engineers for private construction.

Labor market imperfections and public interventions are important factors in determining the availability of people and skills in the workforce. Even more important are the changes occurring in the demographics, the size, age, education, participation rates, and so forth, of the working population. These changes will bear directly on the nature of the workforce available to design, operate, maintain, or manage the new technologies.

CHANGING COMPOSITION OF THE WORKFORCE

The Bureau of Labor Statistics (BLS) estimates that between 1979 and 1995 the civilian labor force in the United States will grow by roughly 25 percent, from 102 million to 128 million workers. The distribution of these workers by sex and age is shown in Table 2. The participation of women in the labor force is expected to continue to increase over this period.

TABLE 2.   Labor Force Distribution (in Percent) by Age and Sex 1979 and Projected 1995[a]

Age and Sex	1979 (Actual)	1995 (Projected)
Men	57.8	53.0
16 to 24	13.3	8.3
25 to 34	15.3	13.3
35 to 44	11.0	14.3
45 to 54	9.7	10.5
55 to 64	6.9	5.0
65 and over	1.3	1.3
Women	42.1	46.9
16 to 24	11.1	8.7
25 to 34	10.8	12.5
35 to 44	7.9	13.0
45 to 54	6.6	8.1
55 to 64	4.4	3.5
65 and over	1.1	.9
Men and Women	100.0	100.0
16 to 24	24.4	17.0
25 to 34	26.1	25.8
35 to 44	18.9	27.3
45 to 54	16.3	18.6
55 to 64	11.3	8.5
64 and over	2.4	2.2

[a] Extracted from Howard Fullerton, "The 1995 Labor Force: A First Look," *Monthly Labor Review*, December 1980, p. 18.

Although men accounted for almost 58 percent of the workforce in 1979, the BLS projects that by 1995 they will account for just over half (53 percent).

The shift in the anticipated age composition of the labor force is particularly stunning. The percentage of the labor force in the 35 to 44 age bracket is expected to increase from about 19 percent to over 27 percent over the 1979 to 1995 period. This reflects the aging of the so-called "baby boom" generation. Conversely, the proportion of the labor force made up of entry-level workers (ages 16 to 24) will decrease from 24 percent in 1979 to about 17 percent in 1995.

This changing age composition of the labor force has led observers such as Joel Fadem to anticipate that there may be shortages of applicants for entry-level jobs and, as a result, salaries for these younger workers may tend to rise over this period.[29] On the other hand, the increasing proportion of workers in the 25 to 44 age group may result in greater competition for promotion and advancement. If computer-based automation makes the kind of inroads in moderately skilled jobs described in the previous chapter, this is the age group likely to be most affected. Thus, the bulge in the labor force may serve only to exacerbate the problem of arrested careers and job dissatisfaction.

Fadem has forecast other possible effects resulting from these fundamental demographic shifts. There may be legal challenges to performance appraisal systems, sex discrimination suits initiated by both men and women, reduced employee commitment to company objectives because of lack of opportunity, formation of lower-management professional associations (or unions) to consolidate and advance their interests, emergence of an adversarial climate within and between lower-management grades, greater pressures to accelerate the retirement of older workers, and agitation for higher wage rates and special benefits for more senior employees to compensate for restricted upward mobility and to restore differentials arising from the increased salaries of younger workers.[29]

It is anticipated that these underlying demographic trends will have an impact on the education level of workers over the next decade as well. The percentage of workers with bachelor's degrees continues to increase over time. As of 1981, 40 percent of workers between the ages of 25 and 64 had completed 1 or more years of college, almost double the percentage in this category just a decade earlier. This rapid increase in the number of college-trained workers does not appear to have been driven by a similar increase in the number of jobs requiring a college education. Fadem reports that the number of college graduates holding blue collar jobs more than tripled between 1970 and 1976. The BLS has estimated that by 1990, the number of college graduates will exceed the number of available technical and professional jobs by 3 million.

While there is no evidence of any change in the trend toward a greater proportion of workers with undergraduate degrees, the relative shortage of entry-level workers and the resulting higher salaries may well result in a decline in the percentage of college graduates continuing on to graduate school. The consequence may be a large body of medium-skilled workers with considerable education, but no advanced or applied training. This is a curious development at a time when the skills required by employers may be increasingly polarized toward low-skilled and high-skilled jobs. If this change occurs, it is likely to shift much of the burden of training workers for more specialized occupations to their employers, either through in-house training or employer-financed outside training. These early-career training requirements will serve to inflate an already growing demand created by the need for career-long retraining to keep pace with changes in the nature of work.

Given the technological changes forecast for the next decade or more, what will be the availability of certain critical skills (engineers, computer specialists, technicians) during this time? Answers to this question may have an important bearing on the rate at which the new technology can be adopted.

ENGINEERS

Engineering is a field that is of great importance to manufacturing industries and is likely to become more so over the next decade. A recent report from the National Science Foundation, for example, noted that manufacturing industries employ almost one-half of all engineers in the nation, with the highest concentrations in electrical, mechanical, and industrial engineering.[30] In recent years the annual rate of increase of electrical and mechanical engineers has averaged about 4 percent, while for industrial engineers the figure has been about 25 percent. When compared with the overall rate of increase in manufacturing employment of only 1 percent, the increasing relative importance of engineers is obvious.

Forecasting the future behavior of engineering markets is especially difficult because historically there have been wide swings in the demand and supply for engineers over relatively short periods of time. Figure 6 shows first-year engineering enrollments over the period 1947 to 1981. Periods of rapidly rising enrollments in the early 1950s and 1960s (in response to increasing demands for trained engineers) were followed by sharp downturns in the mid-1950s and late 1960s.

This cyclical behavior results primarily from the lag between the time individuals decide to embark on careers in engineering and the time they actually enter the labor market. Decisions are based on market conditions that may no longer exist at the time of graduation. If outside forces result in an excess demand for engineers in year 1, relatively high wages will attract a larger number of first-year engineering students. In the short term (years 2, 3, and 4) there is little that can be done to increase the supply of engineers, so wages remain high, attracting more and more students to engineering. By year 5, the first of this large group of prospective engineers

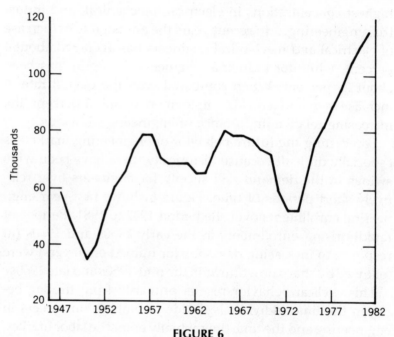

FIGURE 6
First-Year Engineering Enrollments, 1947 to 1981

begins to enter the market and salaries start to fall. These signals do not result in a rapid adjustment, however, because students who start the engineering curriculum in years 2, 3, and 4 (fully expecting to receive the high starting salaries that they observed in year 1) flood the market in years 6, 7, and 8. This may create an excess supply situation, causing wages and available jobs to fall to a level that discourages further entry. The result may be another shortage and, later, excess supply 2 and 6 years down the road.

The complexities of these relationships mean that forecasts of supply and demand in engineering markets must be viewed with some caution, since these lagged adjustment mechanisms are rarely taken into account.

In particular, many engineering forecasts are based upon extrapolations of historical trends. In a labor market such as engineering, which is prone to boom and bust cycles, trend forecasting is likely to lead to widely incorrect estimates of future engineering labor market conditions. Since trend forecasting merely extrapolates from that portion of the cycle that is currently observed, it generally leads to exaggerated predictions of engineering shortages and surpluses.

A second method often used to forecast engineering labor demands, the "manpower requirements" approach, is also prone to error. In using this method, a survey is conducted of major engineering-intensive employers to determine whether the anticipated hiring rates will increase, stay the same, or fall over some future period. The problem with this approach is that employers are asked to specify the number of engineers that they will hire without any reference to anticipated salary levels. As a result, employers are left to assume that salary levels in the future for starting engineers will be similar to those of the recent past (perhaps after making an allowance for the general level of inflation). As discussed before, it is anticipated that labor markets will have adjustment lags and, as a result, that wages and salaries may be somewhat "sticky." It is unlikely, however, that there will be no adjustment of starting salaries to a supply/demand imbalance in engineering labor markets. Because the manpower requirements approach presumes that there will be no labor market adjustment to these imbalances, this approach also tends to produce exaggerated estimates of both shortages and surpluses.

These pitfalls in forecasting future engineering labor market conditions have caused substantial disagreements among knowledgeable observers concerning the availability of electrical and computer engineers over the next decade. At one extreme, the American Electronics Association has estimated that in 1985 there will be more than three times as many positions for electrical engineers as there are individuals to fill them.[29] This study has been largely discounted, however, on methodological grounds. The BLS, on the other hand, projects no shortage of electrical engineers, but that about twice as many openings for industrial engineers will exist as individuals to fill them.[31]

More recently, the National Science Foundation released a study that assessed the supply/demand balance for engineers given two alternative prospective growth rates in the defense budget (3.1 percent and 8.1 percent in real dollars). These alternatives roughly correspond to the U.S. Congress and Reagan administration proposals for fiscal 1984. This study found that only aeronautical and astronautical engineers would be in short supply in the 3.1 percent defense growth case. Given the higher, 8.1 percent rate, there is the potential for a shortage of electrical/electronic engineers in addition to aeronautical engineers.[32]

In summary, there may be pockets of unfilled demand in certain engineering specialities, particularly in aeronautical engineering, but widespread, prolonged engineering shortages seem unlikely, at least at the undergraduate level. There are currently far more individuals in the engineering education pipeline than ever before. First-year engineering enrollments have risen from under 55,000 in 1974 to 115,000 in 1981. The individuals who enrolled in years having the heaviest registrations (1980 on) have not as yet entered the labor market.

In aeronautical engineering, the widespread stories of unemployed aeronautical engineers in the late 1960s (regardless of whether such surpluses actually occurred) are likely to result in a slower rate of entry into this field than might otherwise occur. These shortages will not affect most industries, however, except to the extent that relatively higher wages successfully attract individuals to aeronautical engineering who might otherwise have become electrical or mechanical engineers. Most models of engineering labor markets, however, are unable to capture accurately how much shifting occurs between fields, either during schooling or after graduation, so the indirect impact of prospective shortages of aeronautical engineers on industry through changes in career field is difficult to quantify. Aeronautical engineers account for only about 5 percent of the total engineering population, however, so this impact should be negligible.

The question of whether there will be an adequate supply of graduate-level engineers is more complex than that of undergraduates. There remains a substantial apparent engineering faculty shortage, due primarily to wage rigidity in university salary structures. Being philosophically opposed to paying professors in different departments differing salaries depending on the market conditions in the various Ph.D markets, universities find it difficult to meet the industry-determined market-clearing salary for Ph.D. engineers. As a result, they are having difficulty attracting and retaining qualified engineering faculty. While university salaries have always been below those in private industry, the traditional inducements to academic employment—top notch research facilities and a relatively quiet life—have largely disappeared in recent years. The most up-to-date research facilities are now in industry, not in academia. Furthermore, even the quiet life has partially evaporated as teaching loads have increased dramatically and graduate student assistants have become harder to find. Universities have made some progress, particularly in recent years, toward the establishment of faculty salary structures that recognize the differing underlying labor market conditions. This has occurred partly through direct salary increases and partly through expanded consulting opportunities for engineering faculty members.

If demographic forecasts are correct, engineering may be on the leading edge of a phenomenon that will widely affect graduate programs in the future. As the baby boom generation ages, and entry-level workers become relatively scarce, attractive starting salaries may lure college students away from graduate enrollments in all fields. It is possible that by the turn of the century the problems currently affecting engineering (faculty shortages, fewer graduate assistances) may surface in other areas as well.

The impact of engineering faculty shortages on industry is most directly felt when they present a bottleneck to the education of future engineers who might then be employed in industry. This has not been a particularly serious problem in recent years, however. Despite their concern for faculty shortages, engineering schools have achieved over the last decade the remarkable feat of more than doubling enrollments with only modest increases in faculty size. Indications currently, however, are that the rate of expansion of undergraduate programs is approaching a limit unless additional faculty are found.

Some observers believe that the shortages of graduate engineers will go beyond those experienced by educational institutions. Doctoral enrollments, they say, have simply not expanded at the rapid rate of undergraduate enrollments in the past decade. This behavior is attributed to the decreasing differential between starting salaries for B.S. and M.S. or Ph.D. engineers. This may be an indication of substantial wage rigidity, or it may simply be the result of a preference on the part of industry to provide advanced training "on the job" rather than through independent educational institutions. If there were a real shortage of graduate engineers, however, industrial salaries for starting graduate engineers would be bid up so as to maintain a more or less constant differential with B.S. salaries, but this has not yet occurred.

COMPUTER SPECIALISTS

A second group of workers for which demand will be rapidly expanded in the future consists of a range of professions that are computer related, particularly those that involve software design. The BLS anticipates rapid increases in the demand for systems analysts, computer operators, service technicians, and computer programmers. Responses from industrial representatives in our study indicated that of these categories the skill area of most concern to manufacturing firms was that of systems analysts, which requires specialized, highly skilled computer scientists and programmers capable of designing software. The demand for programmers with lower or more general skills may continue to increase in some areas of the firm, such as in office automation, but process programming for manufacturing is more likely to be done by engineers or designers initially and then modified on the production floor by manufacturing engineers or by the operators themselves.

It is difficult to locate any knowledgeable sources that believe that there will be adequate numbers of systems analysts in the next decade. The BLS, for example, anticipates a 65 percent increase in the number of positions open between 1980 and 1990, resulting in a required addition of 19,000 systems analysts each year.[33] The National Science Foundation study, which aggregates programmers and systems analysts, finds this to be the only category of scientists that will experience shortages in 1987 and also finds that there will be a shortage of this type of individual regardless of whether the gross national product grows rapidly or slowly, and regardless of the assumption made about the level of spending on defense.[34] One person we interviewed, however, insisted that software would have to be developed that was capable itself of writing software, as an answer to the insufficient supply of humans competent to perform the task. Studies of the availability of systems analysts indicate that this may indeed be the ultimate solution to the problem.

The apparent shortage of systems analysts may be partly relieved by a combination of factors. The first is the ability of firms to upgrade employees with computer skills who are not currently capable of software development. This form of upgrading has occurred at other times in the past when there has been an acute shortage in a professional category. It happened for engineers in the 1950 to 1965 period. On the basis of comparisons between the number of engineers in the country with rates of graduation of new engineers, it can be shown that during that time almost 100,000 more engineers were created than were graduated by engineering schools.[35] Obviously, industry had managed to convert a large number of individuals from engineering-related professions to be engineers, without any help from traditional education programs. If the systems analyst shortage becomes particularly severe, firms will act to train their own systems analysts rather than compete in the marketplace for those that are formally educated.

A second factor that may alleviate prospective shortages of systems analysts lies in the prospect of increasing the productivity of software designers. When people talk of software that writes software, what they are really referring to is technology that increases the productivity of software writers. Humans will still have to develop the software concepts, but the actual coding of the instructions may be performed by machine. Furthermore, this new technology may permit software to be modified by relatively simple instructions rather than by completely rewriting the code by hand.

Furthermore, the need for an adequate supply of software designers is being recognized by firms, by government policymakers, and by the public in general. The salaries and prestige of these jobs has increased dramatically over the past decade. Writers of software for computer games, to take an extreme case, used to toil in obscurity for relatively low pay. Some are now being accorded the "star" status given other creative people (such as authors and musicians) through much higher compensation and recognition—their names are often prominently featured in product advertising. Such recognition will undoubtedly inspire many individuals to consider careers in software design.

Finally, the availability of home microcomputers has also made it possible for some individuals to develop assembly language level programming skills and skills in other software development languages (such as C, Pascal, Ada, and Modula 2) without a formal education in this area. According to one interviewee, firms have, as yet, done little to take advantage of the skills developed by more sophisticated users of home computers, but in time this may change.

The problem of a shortage of individuals who can develop computer software is one of quality as well as quantity. Too many of the people writing software today come from a strictly technical computer background rather than from a background relevant to the software application. In the future, it will be even more important that systems analysts understand the processes for which they are designing software. Given the high-level programming languages available today and the prospect of software that can write relatively efficient machine-level code from instructions in higher-level languages, it may, in the future, be easier to make a software designer out of a manufacturing engineer than to expect someone with a strict computer background to understand industrial processes.

TECHNICIANS

Among the lower skilled "technician" categories of technically trained workers, the National Science Foundation declines to predict shortages or surpluses because formal training cannot be used to identify the population available to fill these lower skill category jobs. Nonetheless, NSF does provide historical and projected rates of growth in job opportunities for technician occupations. The results are summarized in Table 3.

A cursory look at these data appears to indicate that if the increases in people trained to fill technican-type jobs continue over the next 5 years at the rate of the 1976 to 1981 period, labor surpluses will exist among drafters, industrial and electrical engineering technicians, and other engineering technicians, while shortages will exist among mechanical engineering technicians. These data should be interpreted with great caution, however, for several reasons. First, there is no reason to assume that the rate of increase in the number of individuals trained in these professions matched the number of jobs created over the period 1976 to 1981. There may be an

TABLE 3.   Projected Versus Actual Growth in Technician
Occupations (in Percent Annual Growth)[a]

Technical Occupation	Low GNP/Defense Growth (1982 to 1987)	High GNP/Defense Growth (1982 to 1987)	Actual Growth (1976 to 1981)
Drafters	0.6	3.3	6.4
Electrical/ electronic engineering technicians	3.0	4.0	6.4
Industrial engineering technicians	1.8	3.6	6.7
Mechanical engineering technicians	2.4	5.0	1.8
Other engineering technician	1.5	2.9	4.8

[a] Source: National Science Foundation.

accumulated backlog for individuals with these skills, or an
accumulated shortage.

Second, the NSF is unclear in its assumptions about the rate
of technological change and its impact on industrial labor
needs. The adoption of computer-aided design technology
may weaken demand for drafters, for example, yet growth is
forecast. Third, there is no reason to expect that growth rates
in the number of individuals trained for these professions will
be the same over the next 5 years as the number of openings
over the past 5. In fact, there is good reason to expect that
supply and demand will be in substantially better balance

than this table reveals, since individuals will generally seek training in areas where they anticipate finding employment. Finally, the training period required for technicians is substantially less than for engineers. Technicians can obtain training more quickly and move more readily between job categories. As a result, market adjustments in the labor markets for technicians should occur more smoothly.

SUMMARY

While it is difficult to identify major skill groups in which there will be an inadequate supply of workers over the next decade (software designers being the principal exception), the actual picture may not be as rosy as it seems. All of the employment forecasts cited in this discussion have presumed that all of the jobs within any given category were essentially the same. If there is a wide range of jobs within any given category, however, it is possible that shortages and surpluses could exist at the same time. For example, there may be an adequate supply (or even a surplus) of electrical engineers, but if a large proportion of those engineers received their training before the advent of microprocessors, they may be unable to take the jobs that are available. This problem extends to traditionally nontechnical jobs as well. Assembly jobs in the future will require workers to use substantially different tools than in the past. Without additional training, a surplus of experienced assemblers could exist at the same time as a shortage of assemblers trained to work in a modern factory environment. The problems of shortages or surpluses of workers in particular categories (as defined in studies by agencies such as BLS) are likely to be dwarfed by the problems created by people with experience in the appropriate occupation, but untrained to work with the tools of a computer-integrated manufacturing facility. The need for redesigning training and retraining programs will extend far beyond the need to shift individuals from one occupation to another.

7

BARRIERS TO THE ADOPTION OF NEW TECHNOLOGY

The inducements to adopt computer-integrated technology are very strong. Manufacturers using this new technology have been able to obtain greater flexibility in manufacturing and design. They have substantially reduced the time needed to design new products and to move those products into manufacturing. They can more easily adapt to changing consumer tastes and preferences and to minority and regional tastes.

Computer-integrated technologies have also resulted in products that are higher in quality and more consistent in quality than were previously available. Information about the product and process is collected and analyzed continuously to catch more quickly the errors that result in product defects. More consistent process performance and early detection of product flaws mean savings in materials costs. Investment in inventory is reduced. Perhaps most important, computer-integrated techniques generate huge advances in labor productivity. Labor reductions in individual systems of advanced automation have been as great as 70 to 90 percent.

Given these demonstrated savings, it is reasonable to inquire why more firms have not adopted computer-integrated technologies and why those that have adopted these techniques have not done so more rapidly. As mentioned earlier, the adoption of new technology is fundamentally an evolutionary process. Currently there are so few flexible manufacturing systems in the United States that their impact on the economy is negligible. Even those firms that have adopted new technologies and are enthusiastically promoting them are only now beginning to exploit them more widely.

The speed of adoption of new technology is limited by a number of factors including the climate for technical change within the firm, investment criteria, attitudes of workers and managers, and perceived risks associated with radical changes in production processes. Before we explore how we might establish a more receptive environment for new technology we need to understand the nature and background of some of the principal sources of resistance in the American economy. These are the factors that control what can be done and how quickly it can be accomplished.

HISTORIC PATTERNS OF TECHNOLOGY ADOPTION

Two features dominate the history of the adoption of new technology in the United States: the increasing division of labor and the development of a confrontationist style in labor/ management relationships. Both of these features of American manufacturing practice are singularly inappropriate to the successful adoption of computer-integrated manufacturing processes. Both subjects were mentioned in our discussion of impacts in Chapter 5, but each deserves closer examination as a major barrier to technological progress in this country. By examining how these practices developed, we may gain an appreciation for why they act as barriers today.

Division of labor

Greater division of labor has resulted from the fact that, as technology has developed, each complex portion of any given manufacturing process has been divided into an increasingly larger number of smaller and simpler tasks. Each of these tasks is more amenable to automation than the complex task from which it was derived.

The division of labor began very early in history, when individuals adopted specific occupations and became increasingly interdependent. No longer was everyone engaged in growing or getting food. Some individuals became specialists in agriculture while others went into trades involving sales, service, or manufacturing. Over the years, manufacturing came to be regarded as the epitome of the division of labor by students of the art of making things.

One of the earliest modern writers on the subject of the development of new manufacturing technologies was Adam Smith. Smith begins the first book of *The Wealth of Nations* by discussing the manner in which pins were manufactured in England in the eighteenth century. He speculates that an individual attempting to make pins by himself might have some difficulty making even one pin a day. However, by dividing the pin-making process into a number of operations, each performed by a different individual, it is possible for a shop of 10 people to produce 48,000 pins in a day. Smith counts about 18 separate operations as part of the pin-making process:

> One man draws out the wire, another straightens it, a third cuts it, a fourth points it, a fifth grinds it at the top for receiving the head; to make the head requires two or three distinct operations; to put it on is a peculiar business, to whiten the pins is another; it is even a trade by itself to put them into the paper. . . .[36]

Smith describes this process of subdividing complex tasks into simpler subtasks as the division of labor.

As tasks become more and more specialized, the amount of output per person increases dramatically. Smith attributes this increase in output to three sources. First, when individuals repeatedly engage in the same simple task, they ultimately become quite good at it. Second, much time is saved because individuals no longer have to switch from task to task, changing their tools and perhaps their physical locations as well. Finally, Smith hypothesizes that the division of labor into simpler tasks was directly responsible for the invention of labor-saving machinery. This is an important observation. As tasks are made simpler they are easier to automate, since inventing a machine to do something simple is much easier than inventing a machine to do something complex. Furthermore, as individuals are given simpler tasks they will naturally begin to think about ways in which these tasks might be performed automatically. For Smith, the individual worker was the single most important source of innovative ideas for developing manufacturing machinery. This is readily illustrated with Smith's story of the boy and the fire engine:

> In the first fire-engines, a boy was constantly employed to open and shut alternatively the communication between the boiler and the cylinder, according as the piston either ascended or descended. One of those boys, who loved to play with his companions, observed that, by tying a string from the handle of the valve which opened this communication to another part of the machine, the valve would open and shut without his assistance, and leave him at liberty to divert himself with his play-fellows. One of the greatest improvements that has been made upon this machine, since it was first invented, was in this manner the discovery of a boy who wanted to save his own labor.[36]

The history of technology innovation in the United States is largely one of an increasing division of labor, making tasks simpler and simpler until a given task can ultimately be handled by a machine, eliminating the need for human labor. It is interesting to note that pin making today is completely automated. One machine performs all of the functions so minutely divided among workers in early manufacturing, and one person tends several of these machines.

The division of labor was elevated to a science by Fredrick Taylor at the beginning of this century. Taylor claimed that increased efficiency could be attained by breaking each person's job into a series of individual motions. He suggested a five-step process for managers to follow:

> First. Find, say, ten or fifteen different men (preferably in as many separate establishments and different parts of the country) who are especially skillful in doing the particular work to be analyzed.

> Second. Study the exact series of elementary operations or motions which each of these men uses in doing the work which is being investigated, as well as the implements each man uses.

> Third. Study with a stop-watch the time required to make each of these elementary movements and then select the quickest way of doing each element of the work.

> Fourth. Eliminate all false movements, slow movements, and useless movements.

> Fifth. After doing away with all unnecessary movements, collect into one series the quickest and best movements as well as the best implements.[37]

This single technique is then taught to all individuals. Taylor recognized that the result of simplification was likely to make workers' jobs repetitive and boring ("an automaton" in Taylor's words). Taylor's response to this was that "The same criticism or objection can be raised against all other modern subdivision of labor...." Taylor merely puts words to the commonly held view that, to be efficient, modern manufacturing technology *must* result in boring, repetitive jobs, because new technology, by its very nature, produces a steadily increasing subdivision of labor.

Managers and other professionals are not excluded from the concept of the division of labor. Their activities have tended to become specialized into the well-defined disciplines of finance, manufacturing, engineering, or sales. These, in turn, have become further subdivided into specific aspects of accounting or scheduling or quality or inventory control or any of dozens of different categories. Only general managers are broadly responsible for coordinating the aggregation of specialists that make up the manufacturing firm.

In the past this division of labor within both worker and manager groups aided the adoption of new technologies. The technologies could be subdivided into smaller increments, and they could be introduced on a piecemeal basis. One operation could be replaced, and then another. Both the worker and the manager increasingly focused on subtasks that could be quickly learned and routinely performed.

Computer-based technology, however, is unlike any of these previous technologies in that it is capable of becoming a *completely integrated system*, not simply a better way to handle individual subtasks within an existing manufacturing system. Thus, computer-integrated technology reverses the trend of subdivision of tasks that has been characteristic of most of the technology introduced in the last 200 years. Instead of breaking the production process into smaller and smaller pieces so they can ultimately be handled by machines, computer-integrated technology brings these many pieces back together again, linking them within a common information system that drives all operations and coordinates their interactions.

In this extraordinary reversal of the trend toward specialization or "rationalization" of jobs, the computer, aided by new communications technology, makes it feasible for the individual production worker to manage a significant array of tasks, embracing many individual steps, any one of which might have been the worker's sole job before the conversion to computer integration. The worker not only can experience a growth in the scope and complexity of the tasks under his or her control, but may also be able to relate what is being done to that which precedes or follows it. Each worker can become an integrator, instead of being the automaton Frederick Taylor envisioned.

This change is so contradictory to conventional managerial and organizational wisdom that it is likely to be unwelcome in many companies. It requires a complete overhaul of job planning and design practices, a change in the way new technology is introduced, and an alteration of many basic company policies and practices. The entire corporate culture is affected. This revolutionary aspect of advanced automation may be overlooked by a management insensitive to the implications of the technical changes, or it may be strongly resisted because it upsets traditional roles and relationships within the manufacturing organization. In either case, technological change will be impeded.

At the management level there will also be a problem of learning to deal with increased integration of the firm's manufacturing processes. Managers, too, will have difficulties adjusting their perspectives. This will be especially troublesome at the time new systems are being selected or designed and built. The integrative aspect of this new technology means that managers must make virtually irreversible large decisions when the system is being implemented. Contrast this with the more traditional incremental approach, in which technological change has been introduced a little at a time. Having made the decision to implement new technology the incrementalist has been able to try a little and see how well it works out. If it does not work out particularly well, it is usually possible to back up a step to the last successful change, determine what went wrong, and take corrective action before proceeding again. Each of the subtasks could be changed without affecting any other subtask, as long as its output remained the same.

Computer-integrated technology, on the other hand, implies the assignment of subtasks to machines and the consolidation of these subtasks into systems under computer control. It is virtually certain that managers will be required to make decisions about adopting whole systems or major subsystems and to commit their firms to acquiring large, expensive, relatively untried complexes of machines. It may not be possible to back up a step or two if something goes wrong. If the new technology fails there are really only two choices: abandon the project altogether by reverting entirely to the original technology (costly in terms of resources and reputations), or commit sufficient resources to make the new technology work.

Some forms of computer-based automation will not be quite so hard on a manager's peace of mind. It is possible, for example, to substitute a single robot for a person at many separate work stations. This kind of automation follows the traditional practice of making incremental changes. The really substantive automation change that forces a revision of management thinking comes with the introduction of computer-integrated manufacturing systems. When the decision to adopt such a system is being faced, it is virtually impossible to try just a little of the new technology as a pilot or demonstration project. The size of the risk can become a substantial barrier to the adoption of computer-integrated systems. In one Caterpillar Tractor Company plant, the commitment to computer-based automation was well in excess of $80,000,000; in General Electric's locomotive plant in Erie, Pennsylvania, the commitment was in the vicinity of $300,000,000.

Confrontationist labor/management relationships

Traditions arising from the development of labor/management relationships over the past century also constitute a formidable obstacle to the adoption of computer-integrated technologies. A review of the literature on the "robber-barons" of the late nineteenth century will quickly show there was little concern for the impact of new technology on the labor force among those responsible at that time for implementing new technology. With the introduction of machinery that could run day and night, there were large costs associated with having that equipment lie idle for a portion of each day. Individuals were commonly hired to work 12 or more hours per day, 6 days a week. Because the level of skill required to operate the machinery was low, children were hired as well as adults. Labor was relatively plentiful and wages were modest. Accounts of the history of the trade union movement in the United States are well seasoned with stories of poor wages and working conditions that served as the impetus for union activism.

Unions provided the necessary political and economic power needed to counterbalance the abuses that were occurring during this period. Unions negotiated or battled with managements to extract concessions for the workers in the areas of higher wages, shorter hours, and better working conditions. In the atmosphere of confrontation, neither managements nor unions gave adequate attention to other issues arising from the introduction of new technology. Decisions concerning new technology were generally conceded by unions to be a management prerogative. Initiatives for worker welfare, on the other hand, tended to come from the unions. At the bargaining table, management's interest in worker welfare often was limited to fulfilling its legal obligations to bargain in good faith. Workers and unions did not share in the responsibility for ensuring that firms ran smoothly; they agreed to follow negotiated work rules.

As long as technological change was largely incremental, these relationships were tolerable. Technological change meant that complex tasks were divided into smaller and simpler subtasks, and these simpler tasks were far more amenable to the development of work rules, job classifications, and working condition specifications than were the complex tasks from which they were derived. For example, the job of writing work rules to cover the number of bolts that must be tightened per hour and the working conditions surrounding that job is much simpler than the job of writing work rules that would cover the very wide range of situations that might arise during the monitoring or supervision of a computer-integrated work station.

In the past, the issues involved in the adoption of incremental technology were largely how many workers would be displaced by new machines and whether the new jobs that were created would be part of the existing union's jurisdiction. While these were often difficult issues, they were simplicity itself compared with writing work rules that cover jobs where the nature of the production process means that workers have to be given more latitude in actions or decision-making. It is possible that the development of jobs in those industries that are now subject to computer-based process integration will follow patterns established in oil refining, chemical manufacturing, and other continuous-process industries. The latitude required of workers in these industries was such that many of the jobs were given professional engineering titles and were removed from the bargaining unit. Moves of this type will be strongly resisted by unions, who will already have seen reductions in their memberships as the result of the productivity gains of the new technology.

Our legacy of adversarial union/management relationships, which is rooted in part in the failure of nineteenth- and early twentieth-century managers to be concerned about the nature of work being created through technological change, thus serves as a substantial barrier to the introduction of new technologies in the current era. This leaves the United States at a distinct competitive disadvantage with respect to other countries (notably Japan) whose labor/management relationships at this point are more cooperative than those in the United States. One can only wonder how the implemention of computer-based technology will fare if we do no better in accounting for human factors in designing and implementing that technology than we have done in the past.

ATTITUDES

During the 1940s, students of human behavior in organizations adopted the biological concept of "homeostasis" to describe organizational reaction to change. They were describing the tendency of a group in which change is imposed to act in such a way as to restore the group to its original state. The objectives of technological change are likely to be thwarted unless organizational attitudes are modified to be receptive to the impending change. In the mind of each person impacted by change there is one dominant question, "What's in it for me?" If the answers he or she receives appear negative or unresponsive, the temptation will be to resist the change. If unity of attitude produces added strength, people with like responses will attempt to join forces. These coalitions may not follow the traditional lines of management versus worker or staff versus line. There may be coalitions of manufacturing organizations versus engineering staffs, or supervisors and factory workers versus programmers and system specialists. Problems with the systems, errors, scrap losses, delays, and added cost may be the consequence. In some cases, the resistance may be so subtle that the search for solutions is kept focused on fixing the technology of the system and not on the

underlying human causes—fear, loss of control, dissatisfaction, or uncertainty.

Attitudinal problems can exist in all levels of the organization. We found middle managers in the companies we
visited who felt that top management indifference toward the
long-range benefits of computer-based automation was a major deterrent to any technological progress in the firm. In
other firms the manufacturing engineering staff was un-
receptive to requests for major automation attempts because
the engineers, who had the competence to make incremental
changes to existing processes, lacked the ability to handle
radical changes. Resistance in one organization was encountered from manufacturing engineers because the technology
under consideration was to be brought in from outside the
firm.

Resistance to technological change can take a variety of
forms. Those who are likely to be hurt in some manner by a
change can *resort to protection under the law.* Employees, for
example, have rights under the Occupational Safety and Health
Act of 1970 to challenge the installation of new technology
where there is a risk of illness or injury because of abnormally
dangerous conditions created by the new technology. Even
where the technology is eventually determined to be reasonably safe, the appeal for government inspection and decision
can cause delays and administrative cost. Other laws have
been promulgated to ease the shock of displacement. States
such as Maine, Wisconsin, and New Jersey have laws providing employees with certain rights that mitigate the effects of
plant closings. These rights include advance notification of
the closing; individual assistance in terms of severance pay,
training, and retraining; and continuance of insurance coverage. Similar legislation has been introduced in at least a dozen
other states in the last 2 years. If greater numbers of people in
both the manufacturing and service sectors experience tech-

nological displacement, it is likely that there will be further resort to legal constraints that limit the discretion of the firm or that impose penalties for certain modes of corporate conduct.

Collective bargaining can become a major weapon in employee resistance to technological change. As increases in productivity have occurred through improvements in processes, there has been a tendency for unions to try to protect the jobs being threatened. At the same time, managements have otherwise been quite conciliatory, desiring a smooth transition to the new technology. In this climate of mutual concern, deals have frequently been struck that have preserved traditional job staffing levels despite reductions in the actual work content. When this is repeated several times over a period of years, workforce levels can become grossly inflated and the magnitude of the needed adjustment can be disturbingly large. A. H. Raskin has described the consequences of a situation of this type. The New York Newspaper Printing Pressmens union called a strike in 1978 against the three major New York daily newspapers when the publishers tried to establish appropriate staffing levels for the more automated machines then in use. The strike lasted 88 days; it cost the firms $25 million in after-tax profits and cost their employees substantially more than that in lost wages.[38]

More recently, unions have sought to include terms in contracts that provide some form of participation in technological decisions. Employee membership in technological change committees has become a part of some agreements. Prior to the recent breakup of the AT&T system, the Communication Workers of America had won the right to participate in a labor/management committee on technological change, thus gaining advance notice of impending change and ensuring participation in some of the decisions connected with new technology. The proposed containerization of ocean-bound freight, with its impact on the number of jobs available to longshoremen, was accepted by the West Coast long-shoremen only after job security rights had been made part of a contractual agreement. In 1982, the General Motors/UAW agreement provided for a guaranteed income stream and retraining for employees displaced by technological change. In the same year, Xerox agreed to a provision that none of the members of the bargaining unit would be laid off during the 3-year term of the contract. Agreements of these types tend to redress some of the injury caused to employees by increasing automation, but they also cause companies to hesitate to adopt new methods if the likely consequence is added cost and administrative headache.

Company procedures and practices, while not having the force of law, become an avenue for resistance, not only for production workers but for supervisors and managers as well. Contentions arise over job descriptions, classifications, pay rates, job jurisdictions, and work rules. In chemical and refining industries the shift of responsibility for plant operation from hourly paid workers to salaried engineers served to recognize an upgrading of the work, but it also served to remove work from the jurisdiction of members of bargaining units. The power of a strike to stop or curb production was thereby blunted. The consequences of such moves have not been lost on present union officials, who are aware that they face two potential problems—loss of members through productivity increases and loss of members through shifts in job jurisdiction. As a result, unions tend to monitor changes in job classifications quite closely and insist that companies give incumbent employees training and opportunity to perform the new jobs. Unions are also likely to be attentive to situations involving reductions in job skills and pay grades through automation.

Supervisors and mid-level managers are often caught in a dilemma regarding automation. On the one hand, they are under pressure to reduce costs and improve performance of the units under their jurisdiction, but on the other hand their own status and pay levels are frequently governed by the number of people that report to them. There is a strong tendency in these situations to hang on to extra people, under the pretext of having to continue past practices or of having to provide coverage in case of machine failure.

A more subtle but often effective form of resistance is simply *noncooperation*. The question in the worker's mind is, "Why help them install systems that put me out of a job?" Harley Shaiken has described a classic example of this form of passive opposition to technological change. A new computer-based information collection system threatened to remove the informal recording system by which the senior molders in a die molding shop kept record (and control) of what went through the shop. It would also have provided management with a means of monitoring each molder's performance. The molders' response to the new system was quiet but effective. Not only was the information provided to the new system by the molders full of errors, but the informal recording system disappeared into the shirtpockets of the molders, where it was accessible only to supervisors sympathetic with the molders' cause.[39]

Finally, there is active resistance, in the form of strikes, slowdowns, and even sabotage. Because automated systems require large initial capital investments, the pressure for a fast start-up and continuous operation is great. The mere threat of a strike or other overt act may be enough to discourage management from initiating change. Reports of actual active resistance to the installation of computer-based technology, however, have been relatively rare. Major layoffs had occurred recently in virtually every company we interviewed, yet the firms were experiencing little or no perceived resistance to the introduction of new technology. We suspect that the economic slump was blamed for the layoffs and that forthcoming technological changes were not linked to the personnel reductions. As a matter of fact, it may be that poor economic conditions have throttled resistance to automation because employees have been persuaded that efforts to improve productivity, costs, and quality were essential to corporate survival. It appears that labor unions and workers in general, while fearful of the consequences of technical change, have tended to recognize the need to upgrade American industry if it is to continue to provide any jobs at all.

INVESTMENT CRITERIA

There is a growing tendency for firms to use quantitative analytical techniques to help them screen and select innovative projects for investment. The financial investment criteria in use today may serve to deter the adoption of computer-based technology. A variety of critics have suggested that current techniques may bias managers against projects that do not offer the expectation of rapid returns or are relatively risky for other reasons.

To understand the foundation for this argument it is first necessary to understand the basics of modern financial investment theory. In general, the basic technique takes the form of estimating the costs and likely revenues of a particular investment project over the life of the project. Then the net totals (revenues minus costs) for each year are weighted by how far in the future they lie, and are combined to produce a "net revenue" or "net benefit" figure.

The weights serve three purposes. First, because inflation is a fact of life in modern industrial society, the dollars that the investment will earn in the future are not worth as much as the dollars that are spent now. If, for example, prices double over a 10-year period, it will take $2.00 in 10 years to buy the same quantity of goods and services that could be purchased today for $1.00. To offset the expected effects of inflation in this case, financial analysts would weight the expected receipts 10 years hence by only half as much as they would weight current receipts.

Furthermore, even if it were known with certainty that there would be no inflation in the future, future expenses and receipts would still be weighted less heavily than current expenditures and receipts. One reason for this is that current expenditures and receipts can be decided and known with certainty. Future revenues generated by an investment today, however, are subject to a range of risks. Receipts may or may not equal projections that are made when the investment is undertaken. Most people prefer certainty to risk in financial matters. Future receipts and expenditures are, therefore, weighted less heavily than those that occur in the present.

Finally, even if future returns were known with certainty and there were no inflation to consider, current expenditures and receipts would still be weighted more heavily than those in the future because of the time value of money. Even in a noninflationary world, money can be invested in risk-free assets (like insured savings accounts) and earn a rate of return. If firms or individuals are to give up current funds for investment purposes, those funds must promise a return at least as great as alternative risk-free investments. The investors must be paid more in the future than they give up today. So inflation, risk, and the opportunity to earn returns in alternative ways combine to make dollars to be paid or received in the future worth less in today's terms than equivalent amounts paid or received today.

The weighting scheme used by financial analysts and economists to convert future dollars into their present-day equivalents is referred to as a "discount rate." For example, if it requires $1.10 repayment next year to convince individuals to part with $1.00 today, the annual discount rate is said to be 10 percent. The discount rate applies in the same manner as compound interest. At a 10 percent discount rate, for example, the investment of $1.00 now would require a repayment 5 years from now of $1.61. Conversely, the assurance of $1.00 to be received 5 years hence would have a present value of only $0.62. When this concept is applied to firms' investment decisions, the discount rate is sometimes referred to as the "cost of capital" since it is the amount firms must pay to have access to financial capital.

When the annual costs and revenues from a given investment project are determined and an appropriate discount rate is selected, each year's costs and revenues are converted into their dollar equivalents at the present time and added up. If the expected revenues exceed the expected costs, the project is deemed to be worthy of investment. Note that in general, investment projects incur most of their costs in the early years and most of their revenues in the later years. Since the selection of a relatively high discount rate will weight near-term dollars much more heavily than later dollars, the higher the discount rate, the greater future revenues must be in order to offset the near-term costs. The higher the discount rate used, the more a firm's investment decisions will be weighted toward incremental changes that produce early positive returns.

An alternative procedure that accomplishes the same goal consists of computing the discount rate that will cause future receipts to be just equal to future costs (this rate is called the "internal rate of return") and then comparing this rate to the firm's cost of capital or, alternatively, to an arbitrary rate developed by the firm for the purpose of comparing investment projects. This latter rate is sometimes called a "hurdle rate," since the rate of return on the project must be at least as high as this rate to qualify as a desirable investment opportunity, from the firm's point of view.

Companies we interviewed that were not actively implementing new computer-integrated manufacturing technologies often cited cost as a major factor. These firms had concluded that, when subjected to the investment criteria discussed above, investment in new technology simply did not pay, particularly in a period of slack demand. These assertions have led us to ask if there may be flaws in this commonly used investment decision-making approach.

Critics of the internal rate of return capital budgeting methodology fall into two camps—those that take issue with the level of the discount rate selected by firms and those that believe the calculation of the future revenue stream is faulty. Among the more persuasive critics of the discount rates currently used by firms are Robert Hayes and David Garvin of the Harvard Business School. They note that the hurdle rates used by firms are generally in the 25 to 40 percent range and that they seem to have been rising over the past decade. They cite, for example, a study that found that about 25 percent of American manufacturing companies require that capital expenditures generate sufficient funds to pay for themselves in only 3 years, whereas a decade ago only 20 percent had such high expectations.

According to Hayes and Garvin:

> Such hurdle rates often bear little resemblance either to a company's real cost of capital (even after appropriate adjustment for differences in risk) or to the actual rates of return (net of deterioration replenishment) that the company can reasonably expect to earn from alternative investments. Again and again we have observed the use of pretax hurdle rates of 30% or more in companies whose actual pretax returns on investment were less than 20%.[40]

In short, firms today have a double standard for expected returns from past investments and from future investments. Firms require that future investment projects not only pay their own cost of capital, but help make up for the perceived low profitability of previous investments as well.

Perhaps an even more serious problem with current investment analysis techniques is the manner in which analysts calculate the revenues that accrue from prospective investment projects (even aside from the level at which those revenues are discounted). The fundamental problem is that a firm only takes account of those incremental revenues that are received by the firm as a direct result of the investment. No account is taken of costs that the firm would incur if the investment were not made. If, for example, firm A's competitors are investing heavily in innovative technology that could make firm A's product less competitive, firm A risks the loss of revenues and profits unless it, too, adopts the new technology. There is a benefit to investment in technology that comes in the form of avoiding this revenue and profit decline. This benefit is rarely taken into account in the return on investment calculation, implying that those making the decisions believe that the competitive environment in the next period will be pretty much the same as it has been in the previous period. Even if this assumption appears to be true when each pair of adjacent periods is compared, long-term innovative investments made by competitors will fundamentally change the competitive environment over time. The import of this is that the long-run is more than just the summing up of a series of short-runs.

In other words, current quantitative financial investment evaluation techniques contrast current firm revenues with those that would be earned if particular investments were made. Yet the appropriate base-line comparison is not with the current level of revenues, but rather with the hypothesized future level of revenues that would be earned in the absence of the investment. There may be a substantial difference between these two base-lines if competitors are making longer-term investments in innovative production techniques. Investment strategies that rely simply on standard quantitative techniques will lead to relatively short-term risk-free projects that involve only incremental improvements in conventional production processes. "Safe" investment policies thus become an artificial barrier to the adoption of new computer-integrated technology and may cause a manufacturer to experience a competitive disadvantage with respect to other firms (either foreign or domestic) that are not constrained by such artificial barriers.

Apparently the shortcomings of conventional financial criteria for new integrative technology are becoming evident to a greater number of industrial managers, as may be deduced from this statement from a summary of a National Science Council report on the CAD/CAM interface:[41]

> In the past, many manufacturers attempted to maximize profits by emphasizing short-term payoff from investment, often using cash-payback or return-on-investment (ROI) calculations as the sole criterion. Companies undoubtedly face situations, such as the comparison of projects for capital investment, in which ROI and other strictly financial measures are still useful. At least as currently used, however, ROI is clearly not appropriate for making decisions on investments in new technology.
>
> ROI methodology assumes stability in the economy, technology, labor, and, most important, the marketplace behavior of competitors—assumptions that have proved time and again to be false. ROI simply does not reflect the long-range benefits of integration. It is noteworthy that none of the firms that the committee interviewed mentioned ROI calculations as significant in its decision to undertake integration.

UNDERSTANDING OF PROCESS PARAMETERS

From a technical standpoint, the speed with which computer-integrated processes can be adopted in a given industry depends on whether all critical parameters in the production steps are known and can be sensed by devices while the processes are in operation. Several of the technologists we interviewed admitted to an inability to understand their processes at a level where all the steps could be automated. This is a real barrier and must be explicitly dealt with by those seeking to develop computer-integrated manufacturing facilities.

Many manufacturers, especially those involved in processing natural materials, have not been able to understand or control all aspects of their processes. Papermaking, for example, has had this problem despite thousands of years of experience. In some respects, the problem is similar to that of making a good stew. The basic recipe exists, but even though the recipe may be followed the same way each time the stew is made, small differences in conditions or materials make it necessary for someone to taste each batch and make small variations in seasonings. Similarly, manufacturing processes experience small variations in materials or process conditions that cannot yet be detected by sensors and controlled automatically. In some cases even the causes for the variations are not completely understood.

While some firms have viewed this as an absolute barrier to the development of computer-integrated manufacturing processes in their industries, it would appear from our sample that variability is as prevalent in industries that have successfully automated as it is in those that have not. The automation of the papermaking process took years of effort, and there were some collossal failures along the way. As in the paper-

making industry, firms who succeed in automating their processes find it necessary to collect a great deal of process
information to determine what paramaters have to be controlled. Appropriate sensing and control mechanisms have to
be located or developed, and when the new systems are
installed, a substantial amount of human intervention is usually needed during the breaking-in period. People are needed
to make small changes in the processes and to respond to
problems raised by the computer-driven machinery. This intervention, however, occurs through operator adjustment of
automated controls—generally via a computer terminal—
rather than by the traditional approach of tinkering directly
with the production equipment. The indirect intervention
mode not only gives operators a "feel" for remote control
through the computer, but the computer can also collect and
analyze data on the results of adjustments. With the help of
the computer-generated data, the adjustment processes gradually become increasingly more automatic. Ultimately it is
possible for the computer to make the adjustments itself,
requiring no further human intervention. As operating experience accumulates, more and more open loops are closed; the
process becomes more automatic and the cost and quality
benefits of automation emerge.

Many firms find that the basic knowledge of how the process works is not a prerequisite for starting into computer-
based automation, but that it is likely to be a by-product of
automation. The learning process and the automation process
tend to go forward at the same time. Without sensors and
computers it would be impossible to collect and analyze the
enormous amount of data necessary to understand the process and, on the other hand, without increased knowledge of
the process it would be impossible to obtain more comprehensive computer control. This situation is a significant departure
from the older-style mechanized or "hard-wired" automation

of the past. Such systems were relatively unforgiving if a process parameter were not known before the equipment was designed. The ongoing improvements, now possible through successive optimization steps, are a much more natural approach to process development and provide useful learning experiences for operators and technicians while new systems are being debugged.

LACK OF TECHNOLOGICAL JUDGMENT

In some firms we found serious gaps in technological sophistication between the technical people employed to enhance the manufacturing processes of the firm and the management that was employing them. These gaps appear to be the result of a lack of technological understanding on the part of top management and an inability of the technical staff to communicate effectively with them. Upper-level management may be very reticent to approve complex, comprehensive changes in production when they have little understanding of the new production methods and there is relatively little experience upon which to base decisions.

Many companies are using technological strategies in process improvements, quality control, product design, and information processing as competitive weapons. Yet managements of some firms are so lacking in an appreciation for the opportunities, risks, and barriers in employing new technology that they are causing frustration and concern among the technologists they are counting on to keep the company in stride with technical progress.

Technological judgment involves more than knowing the basic features of a particular technology. It also involves an understanding of how to accomplish technological change.

To say simply, "Automate the line in the foundry," neither guarantees that the best technical alternatives will be selected nor that they will be successfully implemented. Technological judgment entails a feel for technical options and risks and for approaches that make certain the new methods are properly installed and accepted constructively by the workforce. This involves some skill in sensing technological trends and break-throughs in the industry, in judging the technical competence of the staff entrusted with developing or obtaining new technology, and in organizing projects to achieve change. Our sense is that not all top managements are well endowed with these skills and that the lack of knowledge and skills is a barrier to change.

8

CONNECTIONS AND DISCONNECTIONS

The distinguishing feature of present trends in the application of computers and telecommunications in manufacturing is the high degree of interconnectedness of the processes once they have been integrated into the manufacturing system. The new technologies are drawing industrial operations closer together, if not in spatial terms certainly in terms of time, information, and interdependency. Each step in a manufacturing system no longer stands separate with a life of its own that can be treated as if it were a microcosm of the factory itself. It no longer is self-contained in terms of its own operators and its own inventory, carefully buffered to allow variations in output without serious consequence to the remainder of the system. It no longer has its own independent operating information system.

The events that take place at one process station of a computer-integrated manufacturing system have an immediate bearing in terms of seconds or minutes on what is about to happen at a subsequent station. Also, the events at any process station are determined by what the computer understands must be done and by what the computer commands that machine to do. Thus, the bond between machine and machine exists because of an even more intimate bond between machine and computer.

Similar closely knit computer-based relationships, but involving somewhat longer time intervals, even go beyond corporate boundaries, tying supplier, producer, and customer together in interdependent, interactive linkages. In most of these instances, however, these are information interconnections only; the direct process control aspect found within the plant tends not to extend beyond the firm.

For the individual in the industrial organization, however,

the consequences of computer-centered technological change are just the opposite. Integration of machines has meant the removal of the person from direct involvement with the process. In many cases, because of the enormous increases in productivity that accompany computer integration of processes, the removal of the person from the process is total and permanent. In other cases, the removal is qualitative, in the sense that the nature of the job, the skills required, and the scope of responsibility are greatly changed. The first type of disconnection is that of technological displacement and/or loss of employment. The second form of disconnection is a decreased direct tangible involvement with the process, and a shift to individual, as opposed to group, responsibility for a significant portion of the manufacturing system. Individual responsibility in this instance carries with it the connotation of separation. Gone is the peer group with shared responsibility and minimal accountability. Each person, instead, must operate as the sole provider of whatever is his or her responsibility, often physically remote from others involved elsewhere in the system.

There are possiblities for other forms of human disconnections, however. It is highly likely that there will be serious mismatches between the requirements of jobs as determined by designers of the technology and the skills and expectations of people available for the jobs. Even if people come to the new technology with the right training and attitudes, the design of the jobs they receive may serve to alienate them from the goals of the firm. Appropriate job design, then, becomes one of the chief strategies for assuring that computer-based automation is welcomed by those who have the opportunity to work with it. The next chapter is devoted to a discussion of positive approaches to job design. In that discussion it will become evident that, to create well-designed jobs, there will have to be much greater cooperation among managers, engineers, human resource planners, and workers than has been characteristic of traditional relationships.

As has been discussed in earlier chapters, the consequences of computer-based automation are not restricted to factory workers. The impacts will be felt in various ways by all members of the manufacturing organization. Specialized staff support organizations will see their functions combined with those of other groups, the composite organizations will be smaller, and the professional person in such integrated groups will be an integrator and not a specialist. Battles to protect turf, professionalism, status, and identity will make such transitions in all but the most enlightened organizations a formidable challenge.

Middle management ranks will be thinned. Especially vulnerable will be those managers who function primarily as intermediary communicators, amassing information and/or instructions and passing them on. In the resulting streamlined organizational structure, there will be increasing separation of managerial and supervisory roles as short-term operating decisions are forced down into lower ranks and strategic planning and policy making receive greater attention from top-level managers.

Technical and administrative personnel will thus face similar threats of disconnection in terms of displacement and increasing individualization of responsibility. They may be threatened, too, by mismatches between available skills and needed skills, by restrictions in their growth and development, and by underutilization and isolation.

Even though these undesirable, disturbing consequences are probable if past trends and attitudes are maintained, they are not inevitable. Changes can be made, and there will be managements with courage and conviction that lead the way to new working relationships. Just as with blue collar workers' jobs, appropriate design of professional and staff jobs and organizational structures can provide a positive human environment for technological change. These forms of job design are as critical as are those for the factory worker. Innovative restructuring of work and training to provide required skills will be needed for technical and support staff, managers, and supervisors.

Displacement, the more permanent type of human disconnection, requires other approaches. Even displacements that are handled within the firm will bring problems. The greater issues, however, arise from those displacements that involve temporary or not-so-temporary unemployment. There are constructive strategies for coping with displacement problems, strategies that create an environment of opportunity, competent assistance, and personal security for people in transition.

A variety of means will be needed to deal with displacement. Information about available work and available workers is a prime requisite. Training is another. Assistance in getting to new jobs may be needed. If the amount of work to be done becomes permanently less than the amount of work available, given normal rates of economic growth, some forms of work-sharing may be the answer. These and other strategies will be developed more fully in subsequent chapters.

When we turn from the issues raised by computer-based technology to search for ways to provide a receptive climate for technological progress, we recognize that all that can be done in this volume is to make suggestions that may stimulate others to thought and action. The scope of the subject is so great that it is impossible to provide recipes or strategems for the myriad situations that will exist. Neither do we pretend to know all the answers. Most of what we propose is not completely new nor is it all untried. Credit for almost all of the ideas should go to others who have sought to find answers to these types of problems over several generations of technological changes.

Before we (or others, for that matter) undertake to prescribe remedies, we should make clear the principles on which our recommendations rest. If policy makers lack a coherent set of principles, it is unlikely that coherent policies and actions will emerge. Almost every firm has its own examples of mutually inconsistent policies or practices. We know of at least one firm, for instance, that espoused a piece-rate incentive system but then established a limit on what a worker could earn under the system. Somehow, this firm failed to set out its principles before setting up its practices.

Here, then, are principles we believe should be applied to solving the human problems of computer/telecommunications technology in manufacturing. These principles can guide private and public policy toward better utilization, not just of our technological resources but of America's greatest resource, its people.

The first principle is that *policies can shape technologies and policies can guide technologists*. There is no such thing as a technological imperative. The technologist who says, "It can only be done the way I have designed it," is either stubborn, ill-trained, or lazy. Managers, workers, and educators all need to impress on the engineering profession that it has a primary responsibility for the creation of jobs, and that this creative process should follow principles of good job design that are just as important as the principles of good process design.

Changes should be undertaken as a shared responsibility in which managers, staff personnel, engineers, and workers participate. Such arrangements require openness, ample communication, and trust. The means of developing these qualities in the human relationships in manufacturing will require as much attention as any other aspect of corporate technology strategy.

As participants in shared responsibilities, *all who are involved should also share in the opportunities and rewards afforded by the new technologies.* None of the participants in change should see their contributions used to gain privilege or disproportionate reward for others.

Preparation of people to handle new skills requirements in work must have national priority. It must engage the attention of educators at all levels in our formal school systems. The task cannot be dealt with solely by trainers and human resource development specialists serving industry. An important aspect related to this principle is the need to create an awareness of the kinds of skills that will be needed by all individuals preparing for or now holding jobs where major technological changes are likely to occur.

Large-scale adoption of computer/telecommunications technology in manufacturing will involve widespread displacement of people from present jobs. Although some believe the improved competitiveness of firms will result in such expansion of business that there will be no workforce reductions, it is more realistic to expect that there will be a great many people who will experience at least temporary unemployment.

If the great improvements in productivity do result in labor reductions that outstrip the ability of the economy to create jobs to absorb displaced workers, we should not regard the ability to produce more goods with fewer workers as a tragedy. It is, instead, a challenge to develop policies that ensure that there is an equitable participation in work and income. Equal opportunity for persons seeking employment or advancement has become generally accepted in principle, if not in practice. For persons who have become unemployed through technological displacement the concept of an earned right to work could guide both private and public schemes for dealing with labor surpluses.

Easing the frequent and traumatic transitions from one job to the next becomes a matter of urgency for both private management and public policy making. Failure to attend to this particular aspect of technological change will generate forces that slow progress. In an economic climate of world-wide industrial competition and rapid transfer of technology, slow response to the technological opportunities available can mean rapid erosion of American industrial strength.

At the very least, *this country needs an efficient job information and placement assistance system.* It is interesting to note that the same generic computer/telecommunications technology that will be causing widespread job displacements can provide that much-needed service. It may be time to question the appropriateness of having private local placement agencies that restrict job information and placement activities and to examine alternatives for national systems to perform this task with minimum harm to the individual and minimum cost to society.

The financial evaluation of strategic alternatives should take into account both the long-term consequences of taking a given course of action and the long-term consequences of not taking that action. In a climate of vigorous international competition, it is not reasonable to assume a business-as-usual posture regarding future income and profitability.

We must recognize that *these great new technologies represent enormous opportunities for better jobs and for higher quality of life.* These opportunities will not be achieved without concerted effort, intelligence, and good will. There must be a willingness to break with traditional industrial philosophies, to create new working relationships within industrial organizations, and to establish new meanings for the concept of work. This calls for a spirit of innovation and experimentation, rather than a spirit of defeat or fear.

Above all, when putting forth policies to encourage smooth adjustments to new technology, we must not lose sight of the *importance of the job-creating role of private industry*. Public policies and public activities cannot by themselves produce employment where jobs do not exist. Conditions that stimulate the growth and health of private enterprise will be essential to all strategies for facilitating technological change.

These principles may be criticized by some as being no more controversial than motherhood or the flag. We welcome all who share such opinions. If people were willing to act according to these principles, the task of achieving change would be immeasurably eased. Our real concern is for those who believe that principles of this kind are too visionary, too impractical, or too threatening to a *status quo*. People who share these opinions may be the same people who make it impossible for anyone to enjoy the benefits promised by the new technologies.

Having set forth our principles, what strategies are there to deal with changed jobs, displacement, new relationships, and old traditions? The next four chapters deal with specific areas of concern and possible alternatives for private and public action.

9

JOBS DESIGNED FOR NEW TECHNOLOGIES

Companies adopting new computer/telecommunications technology can choose one of two job design strategies. Each carries its own risks. The first of these strategies can be termed a default strategy, because it continues the traditional industrial philosophy calling for a reduction of the skill level in each job to the very lowest point. Machines designed in accordance with this philosophy satisfy few of the commonly recognized human needs. They may not even match the skills makeup of an existing workforce. People in the jobs thus created are underutilized, and their motivation to contribute more than a barely acceptable minimum is suppressed. The consequent frustration and alienation of people who are capable of doing more but denied the opportunity is unlikely to produce the kind of responsible behavior that is called for from individuals working with computer-based technology.

The second approach, which is the more appropriate strategy, is to design the human jobs at the same time as the technology is being designed or selected, employing principles of job design that satisfy both human needs and requirements for optimum operation of the technology. If this direction is taken, jobs in new manufacturing systems will call for more, rather than fewer, skills. These skills will include "systems" skills—conceptualization, visualization, communication, statistical inference, and so forth—that complement the computer/telecommunications technology. There will be opportunity for human development and growth in capabilities on the job, and the work will provide meaning, dignity, and worth to a person's employment.

There is an enormous difference between the job of the paper mill worker who is so involved with the computer and machine that quitting time is an unwelcome intrusion and the job of the machine operator who must watch a machine go through its paces for 7½ hours and be needed only once during that entire period. The essential difference is in the design of the job, not in the technology that is available.

The risk entailed in this second approach is that the present workforce of the firm—the people available to fill the jobs in the new manufacturing system—will not have the requisite skills to perform the jobs. If a firm has pursued a course of increasing the division of labor for many years, the shift from traditional jobs to new jobs may be too great a step for its employees to take unaided. For the firm concerned about maintaining the loyalty and good will of its workforce through stable employment practices, this undoubtedly will mean an investment in employee training and development. It will also present a considerable challenge to the human resource development staff of the firm, because the types of skills that require cultivation are not those that are the conventional subjects of training courses.

The greatest challenge, however, remains for manufacturing managers. Not only must they reverse the precepts about the nature of work held by generations of managers, but they will also have to revise their concepts about the relationships between workers and managers. When individual responsibility becomes a key skill requirement for employees, managerial behavior and attitude will have to reflect a realization of this change through organizational realignment, improved communications, and, above all, trust.

These changes represent a formidable hurdle for American management. The hurdle becomes even more difficult when the manager's own job is also in transition or may be threatened with extinction because of the new technology. It is difficult enough to change direction if one is propelled by the momentum of conventional thinking, but the strains will really begin to show up when managers discover that the ground beneath them has turned to thin ice.

THE NATURE OF JOB DESIGN

Virtually every job in a factory is designed. That is, someone determines what is to be done, what tools and equipment are needed, what methods are to be employed, and what type (or classification) of person is to do the work. As Davis, Canter, and Hoffman found in a study reported in 1955,[42] the typical job planning procedure is as follows:

1. The overall manufacturing process is planned.
2. The process is subdivided into operations according to various criteria.
3. The operations are subdivided into elements.
4. The elements are organized into specific tasks.
5. The specific tasks are combined into individual jobs.

The dependency of the design of the worker's job on the process technology is clear in this sequence. Consideration of human factors in the design of the individual jobs in step 5 were largely restricted to making sure that the worker had minimal influence on the outcome of the process. Their study concluded that the primary criterion of conventional job design was to minimize the immediate costs of performing the required production operations. The job design guidelines for satisfying this criterion were listed as follows:

1. The content of individual tasks is specified:
    a. So as to achieve specialization of skills.
    b. So as to minimize skill requirements.
    c. So as to minimize learning time or operator training time.

    d. So as to equalize and permit the assignment of a full work load.

    e. In a manner which provides operator satisfaction. (No specific criteria for job satisfaction were found in use.)

    f. As dictated by considerations of layout of equipment or facilities, and where they exist, of the union restrictions on work assignment.

2. Individual tasks are combined into specific jobs so that:

    a. Specialization of work is achieved whenever possible by limiting the number of tasks in a job and limiting the variations in tasks or jobs.

    b. The content of the job is as repetitive as possible.

    c. Training time is minimized.

Responsibility for job design in almost all instances was handled either by engineers (including industrial engineers) or by production foremen.

This traditional approach to job design has changed little over the years, despite a much more general recognition that jobs designed in such a fashion have not, in the long run, yielded the best results in terms of cost, output, quality, or employee satisfaction.

The advent of computer/telecommunications technology, the increased competitiveness of product markets, and the changing demographics of the workforce all dictate a new criterion for job design: Treat each human and machine task in such a way that the capabilities of both person and machine are used to the fullest. This approach is in direct opposition to the "maximize by minimizing" tradition.

The concept of utilizing the maximum capabilities of both the person and the technology implies that there must be some sort of interplay between human aspects and technological factors at the very start of the process design sequence. It implies that at the time the process is being designed or selected there may have to be deliberate trade-offs between the positive human attributes (e.g., ability to sense problems) and those of a machine (consistency, speed). Compromises will be necessary, just as a machine designer must compromise now among machine characteristics. This latter type of compromise is taken for granted by the practical designer, who is readily able to make balanced decisions among attributes such as strength, speed, precision, reliability, and cost. Unfortunately, few designers are even aware that they should be concerned with more than the most rudimentary principles of human involvement with machine systems. For the most part, the concepts of human factor trade-offs or of maximizing the use of human capabilities are foreign to them.

Because it is the human perspective in technological design that has largely been overlooked, it needs attention. New studies are needed. The studies of the 1950s and 1960s opened up the subject and encouraged experiments that have become benchmarks, but the technologies of the future will be sufficiently different in nature from those of two decades ago that the lessons of the past may not give good answers. More specifically, they may not give *complete* answers. The great flexibility of computer-controlled machines, the integrative power of inexpensive, high-capacity computers, and the enormous data handling capabilities of new communications networks were not available for experimental organizational designs 20 years ago. They are available now, and the studies should be under way.

DESIGN PRINCIPLES

As a guide to those who are willing to experiment, and as a spur to those who have not even contemplated the possibility, we offer some preliminary suggestions for job design for computer-based technology. These ideas will be elaborated, eliminated, or emulated as experience dictates, but they constitute a starting point.

To obtain optimal performance from the total person/machine system, we believe the characteristics of good job design should include:

Absence of hazards and excessive physical demands

Computer-integrated manufacturing systems offer unprecedented opportunities to reduce the need for human beings to be in workplaces where there are high levels of risk. The change possible in these jobs is not only important from the standpoint of health and safety, but it also makes possible more equal job opportunities between men and women and for physically impaired people as well.

Worker participation in planning, setting goals, and improving the process

The worker should have a say in how the job is structured, either directly or through representatives. Those who have tried involving workers in technological planning and selection have found, often to their surprise, that workers' perspectives are highly valuable in spotting weaknesses in a given design or in suggesting elegant solutions to theoretically difficult problems. Workers often have a much more intimate knowledge of current process shortcomings than anyone else in the plant. It is a waste of potentially valuable information not to consult them.

Sufficient information in the production system at all times to permit each individual to orient his/her actions for best overall system performance

The importance of having good information may be as simple as needing to be able to decide when to shut down a machine to make a tool change. It may be as complex as needing to know when the supply of a given raw material will run out, what product to run next, and what programs, fixtures, tools, and materials to order up to be ready for the change.

Designing the system so it provides feedback on how a given stage in the process is affecting subsequent stages not only provides information for making timely adjustments to the process, but also stimulates the worker's interest in seeing that the overall system works well.

Comprehensiveness

Each job should, as far as possible, include all types of activity inherent in productive work. Davis[43] defines these as "auxiliary or service (supply, tooling), preparatory (set-up), processing or transformation, and control (inspection)." To this list we would add another critically important task, *improvement* of the process, the product, and the person. Given the rapid changes occurring in both product and process technology, the worker must be an integral part of the learning curve for that portion of the operation in which he or she is involved. Some of the implications of this principle are discussed below.

Social relatedness

It should be possible for workers to establish relationships among co-workers, technical and support staff, and supervision. They should be able to interact with them at work and to solve problems through group processes. The power of this aspect of job design has been demonstrated over time in a variety of ways. One approach has been the autonomous work group, in which a large measure of the responsibility for work assignments, scheduling, and conduct of production operations is vested in the work group itself. Early examples of this approach include the composite longwall coal mining method described by Trist,[44] the organization of work at Volvo's Kalmar automobile assembly plant,[45] and several less publicized ventures at Polaroid Corporation[46] and General Electric Company.[47] More recent examples can be found in Digital Equipment Company,[48] Ingersoll Rand,[49] and Polaroid's Norwood camera assembly plant.

A second form of group problem solving is the currently popular Quality Circle, a concept imported from Japan, but having roots in the goals and methods of the Work Simplification approach championed in the 1930s in this country by A. H. Mogenson.[50] Quality Circles employ group dynamics to elicit suggestions for improvements and to organize task groups to implement change. Both W. E. Deming and J. M. Juran, champions of improved product quality and process productivity, advocate Quality Circles or task-oriented work groups to deal with a range of production issues.

Almost every smoothly functioning production system will have evolved forms of group accommodation that handle a range of daily problems. Recognition of this apparently normal human tendency and provision for it when jobs are designed would speed the adoption of new technology and increase stability in human relationships in the plant.

System relatedness

It should be possible for a worker to see a clear relationship between his or her activities and the total productive system of the plant. The relationship between the job and the end product of that system or of the plant should also be clear.

Access to resources

It is surprising how frequently companies fail to appreciate the importance of readily available tools, materials, information, training, and other resources needed by a person to perform satisfactorily all aspects of a job. Firms that specialize in home appliance service and repair make certain that their repair trucks are furnished with all the tools and parts needed for normal repair jobs. They cannot make money if the service person must return to the shop each time for a part or a tool.

The shutdown of a computer-integrated manufacturing system for as much as 15 minutes can cause the loss of thousands of dollars of production. It makes sense that operators who are on the spot when failure occurs should at least be capable of making simple adjustments that often will restore a system to operation. Discussions with workers in newly formed Quality Circles have frequently revealed that productivity losses attributed by management to worker inefficiency have, in fact, been due to missing or improper materials, lack of tools, improper machine adjustments, or similar problems that were the responsibility of some other group outside the workplace.

The computer itself in a computer-based system can become a resource for the operator by providing instructions on unfamiliar procedures, diagnostic information to help solve machine problems, statistical analyses of quality data, and similar aids to make the job both easier and more complete.

Privacy

A computer/telecommunications system can learn and retain much information about each individual in a productive organization. This information is not just the simple, innocuous data on age, sex, education level, or marital status. It can include information on performance-related items like output per hour, per day, per month, per year; peak output; minimum output; trends in output; quality of output; attendance in the plant and at the machine; tardinesses; health; accident rate; performance appraisals; disciplinary actions; and a good many other particulars. The existence of this information and its potential use or misuse by management can be very disquieting to even the most loyal, productive worker. We suggest adherence to at least these subprinciples in the matter of individual privacy:

1. The production information system should not contain data on individuals which, if released, would abridge a person's rights to privacy.

2. It should not collect data on personal performance without the person's knowledge and understanding of the method of collection and the uses to which the information will be put. (Others will insist that this type of information should not be collected at all, that this smacks too much of Taylorism and the stopwatch approach to production management.)

3. Information that is collected about a person or his or her work should be accessible to the person. Where error exists in the information, a person should have the capability of correcting it or explaining variances. It is as bad to have a system that perpetuates incorrect information about a person as it is to have a person give incorrect information to the system.

Opportunity for individual growth and development within the job and from job to job

There should be a chance for personal improvement on the job. Jobs that have a 2-hour learning time cannot have much room for improvement. Jobs that have opportunities for growth are likely to have long learning periods, a situation that traditional job designers seek to avoid. If a job is to be conprehensive, embodying all of the five aspects of productive work described above, it will inherently have a long learning cycle. Whether this has a seriously adverse short-term effect on system productivity depends on the design of the system and the arrangements made for its start-up. With virtually all of the pacing of a computer-based system under the control of the computer, early output problems will tend to center around machine downtime and product quality. If there is appropriate technical assistance available during start-up, the production operator's learning time may not be a critical factor.

In the long run, the greater capability of the operator to manage and improve the system, because he or she knows all aspects of that part of the system, will yield significant returns.

In a similar vein, each job should be designed so that a person can see opportunity for progression from job to job. "Bridges" or career paths should exist for virtually every position in the firm. Regardless of whether a given employee takes advantage of the chance for advancement, the presence of the opportunity is a signal that limits to personal growth are not being imposed on him or her by company design.

Preconditions

If a firm is to succeed in establishing new job designs to match its new technologies, it may have to do more than simply adopt a set of principles of this kind. Every firm builds up a complex structure of policies and practices that determine what can and what cannot be done. Wherever these existing policies are at odds with new job design principles, changes will have to be made to bring the policies into harmony with the plans for changes in jobs.

As an example of policies that may be somewhat at odds with new job design concepts, consider the differential treatment accorded professional employees in many firms as opposed to that given blue-collar workers. The professionals are called "exempt" employees, because they are exempt from the provisions of the Fair Labor Standards Act of 1938. Blue-collar workers are called "nonexempt" because the Act applies to them. The Act was passed to protect workers from employers who required excessively long hours of work or who failed to pay for the extra hours worked. The time clock, with its long history in manufacturing, became the instrument by which companies proved their compliance with the Act. It also, however, has come to signify the difference between those who are paid for the time they put in and those who are paid for their contribution without regard (presumably) to time. Being "on the clock" divides one population of employees from the other, giving no recognition to individual differences in attitudes, capabilities, or worth to the firm in either population. This dividing line not only distinguishes between modes of payment for work, but in many firms it also serves as the boundary for differentials in other benefits and privileges, such as pay for absence or tardiness, length of vacation, tuition reimbursement for college courses, or even in which cafeteria one eats.

It is likely that many situations will arise in the establishment of computer-integrated manufacturing systems where certain blue-collar jobs will become vitally important to the firm, more important than many "exempt" positions. When this happens, it may no longer be appropriate to perpetuate a pay and privilege differential across the time-clock line. Something like this has already happened in many chemical processing and oil-refining plants where most or all employees have been put on salary and the time clock has been abolished. It has also occurred in a few discrete product firms.

Other differentials were removed by these firms at the same time. One firm that undertook these changes 15 years ago has had an outstanding record of employee cooperation in the introduction of new technology. Its success is not due entirely to this one decision, of course. It has consistently had a management that has sought to recognize and develop the worth of each individual in the company, and this change was consistent with that basic policy.

Changes of this kind in corporate climate may be driven by other factors in addition to the changes at the blue-collar level. We expect to see the consolidation of staff support functions to provide faster responses to the production system. The distinction between line and staff in the thinned-down professional hierarchy may become blurred or disappear entirely at the operating level. As these changes occur, allegiances of professionals will shift away from sharply defined functional "fiefdoms," and people will begin to identify with the total product/process system. Comprehensive information networks will facilitate such shifts in perspective.

The transition to system identity will carry with it a major benefit. It will reduce or eliminate the tendency of organizational units to adopt suboptimal strategies that make their unit look good at the expense of overall company performance. One can expect to see spurts in efficiency because of this one factor alone.

The conversion from local self-interest to total systems thinking can be illustrated by a situation that occurred in a large consumer product firm several years ago. All of the raw materials going into the product had to pass through an incoming inspection before they could be released to production. The manager of the incoming inspection department had a sizable crew of inspectors, and he was under continuous pressure from his management to keep the costs of inspection to a minimum. Overtime costs were particularly unwelcome. To keep all his inpectors busy and to avoid variations in workload that would lead to overtime work, the manager arranged to have from 2 to 6 weeks' supply of raw materials awaiting inspection at all times. This made it easy for him to schedule his operations for highest efficiency. It was not until a systems approach to materials was instituted in the factory that it became evident his action forced the company to carry an unnecessary investment of millions of dollars of extra materials. The carrying costs on these extra materials were in the hundreds of thousands of dollars. It became obvious both to him and to his management that occasional overtime to handle peak loads was preferable to the high-cost strategy he had adopted to make his operation appear well-run.

Moves that (a) eliminate artificial and unnecessary distinctions among people performing different kinds of work and (b) direct actions toward overall plant-level or company-level goals will help to create the kind of climate conducive to successful adoption of computer/telecommunications technology. The importance of a healthy corporate climate was highlighted recently in a *Fortune* magazine article describing the "best-managed factories" in the United States.[51] Many of the firms that were cited have adopted policies that deliberately play down differences between managers and workers and emphasize the feeling of "we're all in this together." The positive results of these policies show up in product reputation, market share, profits, and employee loyalty.

As an example of basic policy that defines a corporate climate, consider these statements made by the chief executive officer of a major manufacturing company:

> The idea that industry consists of two warring factions—labor
> and management—is obviously wrong. In any industrial es-
> tablishment all people must be both managers and labor. All
> are managers when they operate a machine, an assembly line,
> a broom, or a punch press, or when they manage the financial,
> economic, and social activities of the company. All also are
> labor. Some operate machines, some operate assembly lines,
> some operate brooms, and some operate the activities with
> government, with sellers, with buyers, and with the public.
> There can be no dividing line drawn between them. All are
> essential to the business and are complementary in their work.
>
> . . . management, if it is to be the best obtainable, must be the
> collective intelligence of the whole organization. No one man,
> or even a small group of men, can have sufficient knowledge,
> experience, and wisdom to make decisions that can be as
> sound as they would be if these decisions represented the
> collective intelligence and experience of the group. The prob-
> lem is to get this collective intelligence and experience to bear
> on decisions as they are made.

These words appear in a fascinating book written *forty years
ago* by James F. Lincoln, president of Lincoln Electric Company.[52] They sound visionary, even today. They were considered completely unorthodox when they were written. Yet
the Lincoln Electric Company was cited in the 1984 *Fortune*
article as one of the 10 best-managed American manufacturing companies. It has dominated the arc welding equipment
market for over 50 years. Its corporate climate continues to
pay off.

For an older company it can be difficult to break through a
structure of established policies and practices, even if they are
now seen to be inappropriate or even damaging to its future
prospects. If the company is as huge as General Motors, the
task might be considered impossible. Large as it is, however,

General Motors has tried over the years to improve both its automation technology and its human relations approaches. Its successes in automation have tended to overshadow its successes in people-related changes. Recently, however, GM has made two moves that step around its legacy of past personnel practices. It has joined with Toyota in forming New United Motors Manufacturing, Inc., to manufacture in Freemont, California, a restyled Toyota automobile that will be sold in the United States as a Chevrolet Nova. This joint venture enables GM to learn Japanese-style management practices on American soil in an environment largely free of its older corporate culture. Even though a high proportion of the workers in the plant are former GM employees who were laid off when GM's Freemont plant was closed down in 1982, the atmosphere is different. Executives no longer have preferred parking, separate dining rooms, and private offices. Instead of having more than 100 different job classifications, workers now are in one of four classifications and each person is trained to handle a variety of tasks. Workers, through their union, the UAW, are committed to cooperate in a program of continuous improvement through group processes.

GM's second move has been to establish an entirely new automotive division, expected to utilize the latest in automotive manufacturing technology. Saturn Corporation is to be a $5 billion investment that will begin turning out small fuel-efficient automobiles in 1988. It will have a labor agreement with the UAW that will be separate from that of the main part of GM. Greater flexibility in assigning work is likely to be one result. Workers within a given job classification will be able to handle a number of different types of work. The new division has the objective of making automobiles that will compete directly with Japanese and other foreign-made small cars. Creating a new corporate entity not only side-steps existing union agreements, but it also frees the management of Saturn

Corporation from the rather substantial bureaucracy of the parent firm.

These moves will be watched closely by other major American manufacturers who are also saddled with legacies of outmoded policies.

Part of the corporate climate that can impose constraints in restructuring jobs are the contract agreements made with the unions representing various groups of workers. Among other things, these contracts tend to draw careful jurisdictional boundaries around job classifications, spell out automatic steps in pay progression, and require recognition of seniority in the selection of people. Flexibility in work assignments and in matching people to type of work to be performed can be important in keeping an integrated manufacturing system operating efficiently. Contractual agreements may have to be renegotiated. Unions have demonstrated a willingness to work out new approaches for the jobs involved with computer-based automation. The secret to success appears to be early involvement of union leaders in discussions of the changes that seem to be needed and a willingness to accept suggestions on the basis of merit, regardless of source.

In addition to setting an appropriate environment of policy and practice, corporate decision-makers must establish the means by which people will be educated and trained to handle the tasks associated with computer-based systems. Workers, staff people, and managers must all be prepared for their new roles. We will deal with this subject in a separate chapter after we have discussed some of the means of coping with employee displacement. There is an education and training component in the displacement issue also, and we must actually confront the question of skills preparation more generally to include all who have or expect to have a career in industry.

10

COPING WITH LABOR DISPLACEMENT

From the standpoint of society, short-run worker displacement is likely to be the most important human impact of computer-based manufacturing technology. By displacement, we mean substantial changes in job duties or locations. These changes may occur in the form of alterations in the type of work performed within a company, they may entail movements of workers between companies or industries, or they may result in short-term or long-term unemployment.

Worker displacement is not *necessarily* bad, particularly in the long run. While all change necessarily involves adjustment problems, the movement of workers out of jobs that have been dangerous, debilitating, or even merely boring ought to be viewed as an opportunity for improvement rather than a deterioration of the human condition. Likewise, the movement of people away from industries that can satisfy market needs with less labor can become a long-term economic gain for the country.

The most difficult challenge facing both management and labor leadership is the question of how to accomplish job adjustments smoothly, with greatest benefit to job holders left in a given industry and minimum trauma for those who will have to obtain employment elsewhere. This is a multifaceted challenge, requiring a complex set of complementary strategies. Simple, one-dimensional approaches are not likely to provide all the answers. In those areas where neither unions nor individual firms can operate effectively, the assistance of government agencies will be needed.

There are strategies available to employers, to displaced individuals, and to government policy-makers to minimize the harmful impacts of labor displacement generated by the adoption of computer-integrated technologies. To satisfy a

190

goal of mitigating the effects of displacement, three specific objectives must be accomplished: (1) those who are displaced must know where real job opportunities exist, (2) they must have a chance to acquire requisite skills for these jobs, and (3) they must have assistance, if needed, to get to the available jobs. The improvement of job information systems can accomplish the first objective. The second objective requires worker training and retraining programs. The third objective calls for job relocation assistance.

Underlying all of the actions that might be taken to alleviate the problem of employee displacement is the premise that there can be a job for every person seeking one. This will be most difficult to accomplish. If we are to come even close to achieving an objective of jobs for all, there will have to be profound changes in social attitudes, values, and behavior of those involved in the transitions.

In this chapter we will consider job information and relocation assistance strategies, the implications of a "jobs for all" policy, and some counterproductive strategies that will undoubtedly crop up. The subsequent chapter will examine the issue of education and training.

JOB INFORMATION SYSTEMS

A displaced employee is in great trouble unless he or she can find out where jobs exist. The function of job information systems is to communicate this knowledge as completely and efficiently as possible. Job information systems take two forms, those that function within firms and those that function across firms. Those responsible for human resource management within companies have an obligation to make certain that their internal labor markets are kept as open and free of constraints to movement as possible. One mechanism to accomplish this is public posting (on bulletin boards, in company newspapers) of job openings at all levels and at all locations. Many companies now have posting systems at the plant level for blue-collar jobs. Because computer-based technology is likely to cause displacement within job categories at all levels in the firm, it would be desirable to apply posting systems as broadly as possible. Company-wide postings that include professional and managerial jobs as well as office and factory positions would provide the most open internal job information system.

If a posting system is to be an effective mechanism, there must be positive supervisory support for people attempting to use it. A firm that is trying to ease its displacement problems must reward supervisors who prepare subordinates for job mobility and who encourage the use of the posting system. Supervisors who treat subordinates as disloyal or disruptive if they seek job changes are serious deterrents to a smoothly working internal labor market.

Another part of the internal job information system is the preplanning of job availability. This is a responsibility that frequently falls between the cracks, because it involves cooperation among human resource directors, production managers, and manufacturing engineers. Information about expected *future* jobs must also be available to the workforce. This would give an employee time to express an intent to apply and to prepare for a new position. Advance information about jobs that are expected to *disappear* is also critical in effecting smoother transitions. There is a strong tendency for people at all levels to hold on to that which they have, finding security in their knowledge of the present job and the human associations involved with it. In the absence of signals confirming that certain jobs are about to be discontinued, many people will fail to take steps to be ready or available for change when it becomes necessary.

It is also important that job information be readily available across firms, because many people who lose jobs through technological displacement will have to find employment in other firms, in other industries, or, in many instances, in other parts of the country. Once a person begins looking for a job outside the firm in which he or she was employed, the search process becomes significantly more difficult. Information from any given source is fragmentary, incomplete, and usually limited to local opportunities.

Better information exchange mechanisms are needed on job availability at community, regional, and national levels than are generally in operation today. Firms, labor unions, professional associations, and local, state, and federal government agencies all have a role in disseminating useful job information. Present systems for providing this information tend to be insufficient at best and ineffective at the worst. Attempts at new coalitions of companies, unions, and community agencies have arisen as a consequence of major layoffs and plant closings in some parts of the United States. These groups have set up regional job-matching services for those who have become unemployed. These efforts have usually been temporary *ad hoc* arrangements, arising because of emergency needs. It is unlikely that many of these will become permanent institutions that would be capable of dealing with long-term evolutionary displacement problems, but the concept of cooperative efforts on a community or regional basis should be studied as one possible long-term strategy. It would be appropriate, for example, to examine those arrangements that have apparently been successful in the short-run to identify what features contribute to success and what kinds of obstacles had to be overcome.

Because the technological displacement effects will be nationwide, more comprehensive approaches than those available on the local level will be needed. There is an obvious role for the federal government, through the United States Employment Service (USES) or a similar agency, but it appears that neither it nor any other federal agency is presently able to handle such a role. At a minimum, the following criteria should be satisfied if a federal agency is to provide constructive service to those who have been technologically displaced. An effective national job information service should provide:

1. Immediate nationwide knowledge of all job openings not satisfied by transfers within firms, wherever these jobs become available throughout the United States

2. Direct and immediate access to this knowledge from any office of the agency in any part of the country. This calls for a large computer/communications network not unlike those discussed in Chapter 2. The technology is available.

3. Sufficient information about each person seeking a job to permit job matching attempts on a nationwide basis.

4. Computer-based matching of available people to available jobs.

5. Use of the data on job openings and displacements to provide accurate signals to public policy-makers, managers, and labor leaders.

These criteria are not currently being satisfied by the USES or by any other government agency. USES offices tend to be places of last resort for both employers and job seekers. It is unfortunate that this is so, because it is highly improbable that any privately owned national jobs clearinghouse can be organized on the scale required, and there is a serious question whether local private job placement agencies, which tend to be utilized by both companies and individuals in preference to the USES, can be at all helpful to deal with displacement on a national level. In fact, because they have pre-empted broader efforts, private agencies may actually have served to impede the job transaction process rather than facilitate it.

Other countries, notably Sweden and West Germany, have successfully established effective national jobs clearinghouses. Sweden's Labor Market Administration (LMA), attached to the Ministry of Labor, is the major source of job information in that country. Private placement agencies are forbidden by law. Unions and employers both have strong representation on the national and regional governing boards of the agency.[53] West Germany has a national program for employment that is coordinated by the Federal Employment Institute (FEI), a self-governing public corporation associated with the Ministry of Labor and Social Affairs. Governed by a board on which unions, employers, and public institutions are equally represented, it has a virtual monopoly on placement services in Germany.[54]

The essential features of any national jobs clearinghouse are the completeness and the timeliness of the data with which they work. Just as an airlines reservation system cannot be operated on partial information or on data that are 12 hours old, neither can a jobs clearinghouse provide service with piecemeal information days or weeks old. It is not unreasonable to surmise that the lack of timely and complete information may be the single most important reason for the lack of effectiveness of the USES.

The question of private versus public operation of a national jobs clearinghouse brings out all of the usual arguments against bureaucracies and/or private monopolies. There are serious doubts that an organization with as little credibility or technical capability as the USES would be able to pull itself up by its bootstraps, and a fresh approach seems needed. One interesting alternative would be for a company such as AT&T or GTE that operates a national communications network to set up a nationwide jobs clearinghouse. Such a firm would have the technical competence, financial strength, and reputation needed to provide efficient service. A second alternative might be to set up a public jobs placement corporation similar to the Postal Service. It seems clear that something better than what is currently available is an urgent need.

ASSISTANCE IN GETTING TO JOBS

There is no assurance that the jobs created during the next decade will be located in the same areas in which jobs are discontinued. If the experience of the last decade is any guide, there will be substantial job migrations. We have seen the decline of the "smokestack industries"—steel, automobiles, farm machinery, construction equipment, and so on—in the Midwest and the growth of high technology industries on the East and West Coasts. In addition, there has been a significant southward migration of industry, partly motivated by the desire of firms to escape labor union constraints. These patterns of industrial movement are likely to be amplified by plant relocations caused by major process changes. It may be easier to put a new process in a new location rather than to refurbish an existing plant. The implication of these factors is that people will have to move to new locations to obtain work.

An efficient job matching system may not be sufficient to achieve smooth transitions in jobs. Relocation assistance may be appropriate, particularly in situations where a job is assured if a person and his or her family can make the move to the job.

The strategies for providing some form of relocation assistance need study, but several alternatives can be suggested. Currently, income tax deductions are available to help cover relocation costs. These provide little help, however, to low-income earners. Tax credits would have the same drawback in that they would be of little value to those who have no tax liability in the year a move is made.

Many individuals who have been unemployed for long periods may have no income, and conventional tax remedies would be worthless to them. An alternative tax arrangement would be to allow individuals to "carry forward" relocation costs to offset future income tax liabilities. An argument for carry-forward can be made on the basis that relocation costs are an investment in anticipation of future income, so the future income stream should be available to repay the investment before being subject to income tax.

Another possible source of assistance, also with government involvement, is to make low-cost government guaranteed loans available to those who must relocate. These would spread the shock of relocation expenses over a number of years and would help to conserve the unemployed person's resources during a time of maximum financial strain.

Because a relocation move is intended to restore a person to wage earner and taxpayer status, the involvement of the federal government in providing guarantees and allowances can be justified as a means of accomplishing a maximum return to both the individual and the government. The sooner a person returns to earning a wage, the sooner the government begins to receive income tax revenues.

A similar argument can be made for short-term (1- to 3-year) federal guarantees related to the sale of a presently owned home and the acquisition of another at the new location. The objective behind all of these approaches is to make a person who is qualified for a job available to that job quickly and at minimum personal sacrifice, even when substantial distances are involved. Delays in this process represent real losses to the whole economy, not just to the individual or his or her immediate family.

Various proposals have been put forward that would allow employees to make tax-deductible payments into savings accounts that would be available to them to defray retraining expenses if needed for a job change. These savings plans, similar to current Individual Retirement Accounts (IRAs), would give the person more latitude in determining his or her own retraining program. It is possible that such arrangements could be set up to be more broadly applicable to a range of possible re-employment costs, including those of job placement and relocation.

WORK FOR EVERYONE

Given the ability of computer-integrated manufacturing processes to displace or replace significant portions of the labor force, the question of whether advanced automation techniques will result in large numbers of more or less permanently unemployed workers has gained increasing importance. Even if we retrain large numbers of displaced workers, will jobs be available to them when they complete training? In the past, the United States economy has shown tremendous resilience in absorbing additional numbers of workers into the labor force. Even during modest recessions, the economy has often been able to generate increased numbers of jobs; unemployment has risen only because the numbers of jobs did not increase as rapidly as the workforce. Thus, our historical evidence would indicate that *in the long run* the economy should be able to absorb the workers displaced by new technology.

There is a limit to the *rate* at which new jobs can be created, however. New jobs are not generated instantaneously, and labor markets adjust to changing market conditions with substantial lags. Furthermore, the rate of increase in new jobs is governed by many factors in addition to the availability of individuals to work. Government fiscal and monetary policies have a substantial impact on the rate of economic growth and hence on the rate of job creation. External events, such as wars and political adjustments in foreign countries, can also have a substantial impact on the rate of job creation in the United States. If we learned nothing else from the 1973 to 1974 OPEC oil embargo, it is that political and economic actions beyond the direct control of the United States can have disturbing effects on the American economy.

If the rate at which workers are displaced exceeds the rate of new job creation, temporary unemployment will result. As the pace of the implementation of new technology quickens, we anticipate that unemployment of this type may materialize. Furthermore, the word "temporary" is somewhat misleading in this context, as it may take a substantial period of time for these changes to work their way through the economy. If this is true, we are left with the alternatives of (1) accepting long-term high levels of unemployment, (2) stimulating the economy in an effort to force it to grow fast enough to create job opportunities for displaced workers, or (3) focusing on a range of alternatives that promote flexibility in the distribution of work, including a shorter work week, a shorter work year, partial retirement for older workers, and job-sharing.

The first of these alternatives—high unemployment levels—means sustained economic privation for what could be a sizable fraction of our workforce. It would be unacceptable both on humanitarian and political grounds, unless all other possible remedies have been exhausted.

Efforts to accomplish the economic growth of the second

option need to continue, but these efforts have only been partially successful in the past, due in part to the government's inability to develop consistent fiscal and monetary policies and in part to the inability of American producers to retain competitive leadership. Furthermore, there is a practical limit to the rate at which the economy can grow. For the short run, at least, it is worthwhile to consider other policy options to help ease transitions.

The third group of alternatives presents opportunities to develop innovative programs to ease the distress of technologically displaced workers and improve the quality of life in the United States. Work-sharing will mean that the standard of living for individuals will increase more slowly than if it were possible to employ everyone fully while adopting the new technologies, but it should have a positive influence on the distribution of income and it should result in a broadening of the country's skills base. It will also help to avoid creating a new class of people that is permanently unemployed or dependent upon the government for jobs or other means of support.

Work-sharing programs can involve shortening the workday, the work week, or the work year. Reducing work hours has been a frequently used approach as a means of temporarily avoiding layoffs. In some instances, as in the depression of the early 1930s, and more recently in the recession of the early 1980s, shortened workweeks became a way of life for people in many firms over extended periods of time. Although unemployment insurance laws in most states act as disincentives to arrangements for temporary workweek reductions, employees have often voluntarily accepted reductions because of the shared nature of the impact and the fact that it involves the least amount of disruption to the firm.[55] Work rotation, in which weeks of work are interspersed with weeks of nonwork, is a variation of the shortened workweek.

Other, more permanent forms of work-sharing have oc-curred in the reduction of the number of working hours in the workyear, through longer vacation periods, more holidays and personal time off, and even through time allowed for "sabbaticals" (periodic extended vacations tried in the steel industry), community service time, and educational or train-ing time. Changes of this kind have already lowered the average workweek in some industries well below the 40-hour norm. By 1979, for example, the number of annual paid days off for a person with 20 years seniority in General Motors ranged from 46 to 49 days. If the person worked 40 hours a week for the remaining weeks, the average workyear would be only slightly more than 80 percent of the time available in 52 weeks of 5 working days each.

Workweek reductions that provide an appreciable amount of leisure may not necessarily produce increased work-sharing. Instead, moonlighting—employees taking on sec-ond or third jobs—may increase, thus negating the intended effect of curtailed hours on the primary job. Poor and Steele found that even when jobs were kept at 40 hours per week but shifted to a 4-day schedule, approximately 20 percent of the workers held second jobs.[56] Simply mandating reductions in workweek hours, therefore, may not accomplish the intended purpose of making work available to more people.

Other forms of work-sharing have involved the shortening of a person's worklife. Increased educational preparation for jobs and life in general has automatically removed many young people from more than short-term employment during the first 16 to 22 years of their lives. Requirements for retrain-ing or continued education serve further to decrease time for work. Finally, permissive or suasive policies regarding early retirement serve to curtail work years at the end of a person's worklife. At the same time that these forces are shortening an individual's worklife, other forces are at work to lengthen it.

Better health, leading to greater longevity, has made it both desirable and necessary for people to work for more years. Elimination of mandatory retirement rules and delaying the Social Security eligibility age also serve to encourage longer participation in the workforce. It appears we are approaching a time of national schizophrenia regarding retirement.

COUNTERPRODUCTIVE STRATEGIES

If our society fails to develop effective positive steps to handle the displacement issue, it is possible that *ad hoc* strategies to counter adverse effects will be adopted by those most directly impacted. Some of these, arising to protect short-term interests, will serve to penalize or halt the technological advances seen as the causes of the problems. The reasoning will be that if workers are being displaced more rapidly than they can be absorbed by the economy, the problem can be solved by directly or indirectly controlling the rate of adoption of new technology. Strategies based on this premise may take the form of restrictions either on firm behavior or on competition from producers using advanced technologies. Examples include the enforcement of union work rules concerning the number of employees required to operate particular production processes (regardless of how different the process is from that which existed when the rule was developed), barriers to closing outdated plants, and restrictions on imported goods produced by foreign firms using new manufacturing technologies.

Furthermore, employees may adopt their own informal strategies by generating slowdowns, work stoppages, or critical machine failures that artificially expand the size of the workforce needed to meet production requirements. Such tactics have occurred in certain industries for years.[57]

Each of these strategies suffers from the mistaken view that the wealth of a nation is measured by its employment rather than by its output of goods and services. According to this view, by focusing on preserving jobs, we improve our economic well-being. From this perspective, the worst thing that could happen would be that someone discovers a way to produce everything that everyone could possibly use or want with no labor at all. The danger of being trapped by this form of illogic can be avoided by measuring our welfare by the output of goods and services rather than by employment. If we generate more leisure time in the process, then the problem becomes one of ensuring that this increased leisure is not localized in the form of unemployment and deprivation for some, and employment and affluence for others.

11

EDUCATION
AND TRAINING

W hether a person fits into the new industrial environment created by computer/telecommunications technology will depend largely on the type of preparation he or she has had for that environment. Two aspects of that preparation—education and training—are properly considered together, because they should complement each other. The third aspect, attitude, will be discussed in the next chapter.

The preparation of people for industrial jobs involves elements that can be provided by the formal education system of our schools and other elements of training that must be provided either by manufacturing firms themselves or by public or private agencies. Education involves the development of a person's general capabilities for living within a society. Training, on the other hand, provides a person with the more specific skills for performing tasks, whether these tasks are at work or at leisure. We think of schools as primarily in the business of providing an education, but it is clear that they are frequently involved in training as well. Schools train people, for example, in typing skills, homemaking skills, shop skills, and computer programming skills. At the college level, there is a similar dichotomy in the curriculum between education for living and professional training.

The forces arising in industry that will play a part in shaping education and training programs in the next decade or so are (1) demographic shifts in the workforce, (2) displacement caused by technological change, and (3) skills requirements of new technologies. The workforce will be 25 percent larger. There will be more women and fewer young people in the workforce. Seventy percent of the workforce will be between 25 and 54 years of age. Job displacement will be a continuing general problem throughout industry. Technological change, driven by innovations in computer applications and telecommunications linkages, will continue to require new abilities of people in industry.

In addition to these forces that come from the labor market itself, other conditions will place demands on education and training systems. For blue-collar workers, the weakening of bargaining power of labor unions will put a premium on individual employee strategies for success. A person may not be able to count on the union to secure pay increases, promotions, or protection from layoff. The health of the economy will play a major role, both in terms of demand for education and training activities to produce qualified workers and in terms of the resources available to pay for such activities. Decisions relative to national defense and aerospace likewise will affect the level of demand placed on the educational and training facilities of the country, particularly for more highly trained technical personnel.

The combination of these factors produces such an uncertain picture at this time that it would be difficult to lay out a precise program of education and training for industrial work. It is possible, however, to identify some of the joint objectives that should be common to any approach to individual development. One such objective is the need for *flexibility* in employees' abilities to move readily from job to job. This capability is being stressed by firms that are revamping their organization of work. People are more likely than ever to be asked to shift from one type of work to another as a normal aspect of their employment. This flexibility may be called upon daily, as a part of the employee's normal work routine. Alternatively, it may occur at specific times during people's careers as assignments and/or technology change. Many firms are emphasizing the need for flexibility by reducing the number of different job classifications in a plant to a very few. The management of a new GE plant that will house a single large computer-integrated manufacturing system plans to have only three classifications of blue-collar workers in the plant. People in these classifications will handle the entire gamut of setup, operating, and maintenance chores. There will be a wide variety of assignments in each of the classifications, and frequent switching of the assignments. Workers will have to acquire the skills needed to perform the range of tasks. Their job classification will be broad enough that it remains unchanged even though there has been a considerable shift in tasks being performed.

Continuing skills renewal and upgrading is a related capability that will also be emphasized. Along with job shifts there will be changes in job content incurred by changes in products, organization of work, and process technology. These changes will necessitate repeated further training if employees are to retain their worth to the firm.

Somehow the education and training an individual receives will have to develop within him or her a sense of *self-reliance and resourcefulness*. This will be a needed attribute for all people in industrial settings where there will be frequent job transitions (particularly those between firms) without much support from employers, unions, or the public. This is not to say that none of these parties will be interested in helping out; it is just more realistic to recognize that none may be able to do as much as they might wish. This has generally been the case in the past, and, with no strong pressures now for change, it is not likely that the situation will get much better with time. Skills associated with self-reliance include an ability to manage finances, to market one's skills, to anticipate shifts in job requirements, and to sense opportunities.

There are at least three different populations that must be considered as clients for education and training in industrial skills. First, there are those in industry that will be asked to move into jobs on computer-based systems. Then there are those who will be displaced because of these systems, and, finally, there are those not in the industrial workforce who are preparing for entry into industrial jobs. These are not static populations, of course, and many people will discover that, in time, they will have been through each of these three states at least once. In this evaluation of education and training strategies we will look first at the requirements imposed on the education system by the new needs of industry and then we will examine the contribution that can be made by training. Following that, we explore what kinds of training programs exist in this country and in countries that have taken the lead in occupational training.

EDUCATION

It should be understood at the outset of this section on education that we are defining *what* we consider to be the skills needs of people who will be operating computer-based systems. We are not attempting to prescribe *how* these objectives should be met. Although both authors are educators, we are not educationists. These needs are presented in the hope that the planners and providers in the education system will be motivated to respond with appropriate programs.

A useful starting point is the list of skills qualifications we developed in Chapter 4. Following these we can examine the concepts of flexibility, self-reliance, and renewal to see whether some aspects of these fall within the purview of education. Other special needs of staff professionals and managers need to be considered, as well.

Visualization is the ability to see in one's "mind's eye" what is happening within the process, based on certain clues (meter readings, video data, oral communications, etc.) that have been received. Reading requires an ability to visualize a situation from the words on the printed page. Radio sports broadcasts and adventure programs rely on the audience's ability to vizualize the scene being described. Given the decline in interest in both of these media and the ascendancy of the graphic completeness of television, we may be providing far fewer opportunities to develop this skill in everyday activities. If workers are to perform their duties at some distance from the processes for which they are responsible, the ability to envision what is happening from the data presented to them will become increasingly important.

Two other skill needs are closely linked with visualization. An *understanding of process phenomena* is essential. The ability of a person to visualize something depends on having at some time experienced the thing in reality. It would be difficult to visualize a football game from a radio broadcast if one had never seen a game played. The same applies to production processes. People will have difficulty understanding the full meaning of information presented to them by their instruments if they do not understand by first-hand experience what is actually going on in the processes under their control. The educational aspect of this skill development is in providing an appreciation of how materials, energy, and machines interact. In the context of new computer/telecommunications technology, the linkages between sensors, computers, and actuators are particularly important. These are the interactions between the devices that sense conditions and inform computers, the computers that evaluate the data and initiate instructions, and the devices that carry out the commands.

Conceptualization requires both process understanding and visualization skills to extrapolate from current information to what should be done. It is the ability to reason in the abstract to the point of making a decision to act or not to act. It involves an ability to decode and comprehend a variety of forms of communication, to draw inferences from information, to consider alternative meanings and/or consequences of a situation, and to formulate an appropriate response. This skill needs to be highly developed in systems operating personnel, maintenance technicians, manufacturing engineers, supervisors, and any other personnel responsible for operating or servicing a computer integrated system.

A very large part of a person's education is devoted to developing decoding and comprehension skills, particularly in reading and in mathematics. It is not clear, however, that there is any systematic approach used in developing conceptual skills, particularly among students who, for various reasons, are likely to become blue-collar workers in industry. Students going on to become engineers or managers or professional staff are likely to have sufficient opportunity to develop these skills in their post-secondary education, but not so for the blue-collar worker.

An increasing emphasis on the use of *statistical techniques* to control processes and to evaluate product quality makes it desirable that these skills be available in at least rudimentary form among production workers. The use of statistics in defining a problem is often an important first step toward solving it. The Japanese have made good use of the fact that their workers and foremen understand and can apply simple analytical techniques as a part of their problem solving approaches. Some of the techniques that are useful include the ability to design an inquiry or experiment, to sample, to organize data, to understand graphical presentations, to calculate means and distributions, to use some concepts of probability, and to understand trend information and statistical limits.

The next two skills requirements are likely to give American educators a great deal of trouble. *Attentiveness*, the ability to concentrate on what is going on for extended periods, runs counter to our culture, where interest is whetted by means of distraction and change. Both our methods of instruction in school and our prime means of amusement (TV) are geared to attention spans of about 15 minutes. Production workers at conventional routine tasks learn to "tune out" to their jobs, relegating control over job-related activities to a few lower ganglia, leaving their minds free to consider anything else of current interest. Jobs associated with computer-based technology will tend to require more consistent attention, because of the scope and scale of the responsibilty. It will be critically important for schools to develop techniques for stretching attention spans and stimulating the powers of ob-servation.

Individual responsibility is a quality that undoubtedly can be shaped by educators, but it is not one that they can handle alone. Of all the abilities we have discussed, this is most dependent on the culture in which a person develops. It requires not only a form of personal discipline but also a motivation to act in ways that are defined (by the society affected) as being responsible.

The drive to simplify jobs to the barest minimum human input has tended to give minimum value to this quality of responsible behavior. Consequently, managers who are look-ing for people to work on new, expensive, flexible manufac-turing systems have to take extraordinary measures to ensure that the people selected can be counted on to handle the responsibilities.

It is not contradictory to expect a person whose job calls for individual responsibility also to have the ability to work with groups to improve the production system. Individual and group *problem-solving skills* have been found by many firms as a way to get at the many small, but cumulatively important, deterrents to product quality, productivity, or lowered costs. Problem-solving approaches exist that can be taught and practiced in schools. The development of these skills would have value at all levels in manufacturing.

Other interpersonal skills that can be developed through education include the various forms of *communication*: written, spoken, and electronic. Because of the degree of isolation between jobs in computer-based systems and the degree of interdependency between work stations, accurate, timely communications will be critically important. Communications skills include the ability to listen and receive information as well as to transmit it. Instruction in communications skills is another area in which the education system tends to fail those who leave it early, or who are processed through its less demanding levels.

Flexibility and *self-reliance* are two qualities that might be considered survival skills, rather than job skills. They are needed, not so much to perform any given job as they are to enable a person to cope with changes when they occur. Many educational inputs go into producing these capabilities, from how to manage a bank account to how to follow instructions. Educators should, perhaps, consider it within their area of responsibility to develop a package of skills that would enable industrial workers to handle with more confidence and efficiency the problems of job acquisition, maintenance, and change. Self-reliant people are able to use the full range of job services available to them in any given situation. With the prospect of many changes in store for them, industrial workers will need a significant measure of this quality.

The reader may wonder why we have failed to emphasize computer skills training. It is not that such skills are unimportant, but this aspect of education is already receiving a great amount of attention. Our primary concern in this area is that such training should be available to those in public schools who will be heading directly into industrial jobs rather than college and that such training should also be available to older workers who have not yet picked up these skills from their more computer-literate youngsters.

EDUCATION FOR ENGINEERS AND MANAGERS

The educational needs for professional engineers and managers in manufacturing are at least as complex as those for the production workforce. All of the skills needs described thus far are appropriate skills for the professional, but there are additional requirements that will challenge the educational system. Colleges, universities, and technical institutes are likely to have big problems in packaging and delivering instruction for these added requirements and still retain the conventional bounds of their current degree programs.

The package of skills needed by the manufacturing manager in the world of computer-based technology is currently under study,[58] and national-level discussions have begun at the National Academy of Engineering on manufacturing education needs from the engineering point of view.[59] Until more attention has been given to the question, any conclusions are premature. Nevertheless, we venture a few suggestions that are likely to be among the less controversial ideas that eventually will be advanced.

Education systems will be asked to provide greater breadth of knowledge for both manufacturing engineers and managers. Each profession will have to have a fairly extensive understanding of basic concepts in the other domain. Engineers will need to know business principles so they can more effectively interface with managers. An understanding of financial concepts such as costs, breakeven, time value of money, depreciation, cash flow, and analysis of investment proposals will be particularly important. Similarly, engineers will need to learn the interpersonal skills of team building, motivation, communication, and project organization and management. Engineers involved with design and selection of machines and production systems will also need to understand and appreciate the principles of human job design discussed in Chapter 9.

Manufacturing managers will need technical competence to understand the processes they will be acquiring and managing. They will have to be able to evaluate the performance of their technical staffs. They will have to be computer-literate, that is, able to use the computer as an information base, a communications tool, and as a means of problem solving. As the chief orchestrator of a continuing series of changes, the manufacturing manager will have to be a master at managing change, using skills that are likely to be at variance with those used to maintain the *status quo*. Manufacturing managers will require superb organizational and human resource skills, especially those related to organization of work, job design, group dynamics, motivation, training, and development.

We have said that the need for faster response to production system problems will require the integration of various manufacturing support functions. If this postulate is correct, the manufacturing manager is most likely to become the integrative person. The manager's role as integrator will necessitate a full understanding of each of the support disciplines involved in the manufacturing plant, especially inventory control, quality assurance, production planning and scheduling, and materials handling. Each of these disciplines has its own principles that will have to be learned. Some of the principles, such as those in quality assurance, may have to be reconstructed in the light of changes occurring because of new technology or because of competitive pressures for higher standards.

Responses to these additional needs of engineers and managers will have to come largely from the post-secondary education system. The evident need for inderdisciplinary instruction will evoke some head-scratching among the professorial purists who are reluctant to see jurisdictional boundaries broken down.

The final service that can be provided by the educational system for all people working with new technology, both blue collar and professional, is the provision of *continuing education* for skills renewal and upgrading. The dynamics of technological change will be at the root of pressures for added education. The problem for educators will be to keep abreast of, or even anticipate, technological developments, so they can offer courses that are up-to-date and helpful.

WORKER RETRAINING

Retraining is an area that has received increasingly more attention over the past few years as it has become clear that many of the individuals laid off in the recent recession will never be able to return to their old jobs. Retraining will also gain increasing importance in equipping people presently employed with the skills to handle computer/telecommunications technologies.

Retraining programs can be separated into two categories that might be characterized as "demand-pull" and "supply-push." Demand-pull retraining programs occur when employers recognize that individuals with specific kinds of skills will be needed in the immediate future. For example, when a firm anticipates opening a new plant with the latest computer-integrated technology, the employees who are to operate the new plant will generally have to be given extensive training in its operation and control. Appropriate training up front, before the new technology is installed, is critical both because employees must be able to operate the new control systems efficiently and because of the positive effect training can have on attitudes of workers. In order for the implementation of new processes to be successful, employees must view these processes as new tools, not as a threat to their own job status or security. One manager we interviewed, whose firm had, until recently, experienced mixed success with computer-integrated manufacturing, summed the situation up this way:

> The biggest issue . . . was getting the people attuned that this monster . . . wasn't going to be added work—that it was actually going to benefit them. [This gets into] the whole business of involving the user and having him part of the activity with very extensive training. We blew this a couple of years ago. . . . We did it in an aborted start and never got the user involved. This time we really did it right, and we have a package that everybody just can't wait to [get started with].

Demand-pull retraining is an area that firms have historically handled relatively well, but the requirements for training programs will change as the technology evolves. One manufacturing vice president suggested that with the more rapid introduction of new product changes, it would become necessary to retrain the workforce continuously. In short, company-sponsored continuing training and education programs will be as necessary for the factory workforce as for research and development personnel.

In addition to being driven by rapidly changing products and production processes, company retraining programs will be needed to maintain high levels of machine utilization. Because the pool of workers in any particular job category will be smaller, worker absences for vacations or illnesses will have a larger impact on firms than in the past. One way to keep machines going will be to develop workers that are skilled at more than one job. Companies may then be able to flexibly reassign people within the factory. Along this line, some firms have set up worker qualification programs where employees receive additional training and can earn titles such as "qualified solderer." Those employees who can be assigned to a variety of jobs because of their capabilities are then compensated at a higher rate than those who can perform only one function.

One company has set up a printed circuit board plant where all of the production workers are trained to run each of the 23 different operations in the process. Each person is tested in each operation to qualify as a full-fledged member of the production team. In this plant, workers are expected to move on their own from operation to operation during every day as bottlenecks develop or as absences occur.

If jobs associated with computer-based technology are established according to the principles outlined in the chapter on job design, the content of demand-supply training programs will have to encompass a wider range of subject matter than is currently the standard fare for in-house training. For many companies, the skills listed under the education section will have to be introduced in training sessions for employees about to move into computer-integrated manufacturing jobs. These efforts would be in addition to the job-specific training that must be provided. Some companies have introduced training courses in communications skills, machine processes, computer use, statistics, and group problem-solving. Few, if any, have tried to develop the more elusive qualities of individual responsibility, self-reliance, or conceptualization. Managers and trainers will both be taxed to find ways to enhance the caliber of their workforce in these characteristics.

RETRAINING OF DISPLACED EMPLOYEES

Supply-push retraining occurs when employees lose their jobs as a result of being displaced by new technology and then receive training to prepare them to begin new careers. Supply-push retraining programs have met with only limited success because of a number of factors. First, employee expectations are often high relative to available jobs. It is difficult for a person such as a steel worker accustomed to earning $18.00/hour to adjust to the need to enter a 6-month training program to qualify for a job at $8.00/hour. Such people tend to exhaust all avenues of re-employment in their old occupation before seeking new forms of work. Unfortunately, by the time individuals have been unemployed a long time, they often have become demoralized and their attitudes themselves are barriers to successful education. Furthermore, in most cases at least a part of the retraining cost must be borne by the trainees themselves. When these individuals finally decide they must obtain training to take lower-paying jobs, they generally have little money to spare and are not perceived as being good credit risks by lending institutions.

Because these are supply-push retraining programs, there is a tendency to overlook the serious question of whether individuals are being retrained for jobs that will actually exist. As a practical matter it is difficult to identify today large categories of currently available jobs that individuals with little formal technical background can be readily trained to fill.

There is little that firms can do, by themselves, to facilitate supply-push retraining. Although some companies have set up retraining programs for laid-off workers as part of their separation package, the range of expertise that is required to develop a successful supply-push retraining program is beyond the means of most firms. Successful programs depend on identification of future employment opportunities for displaced workers, career counseling that includes an evaluation of the capabilities of potential trainees, qualified instruction, and a means of supporting displaced workers during the training period. The success of these types of programs depends upon close cooperation between firms, unions, government authorities, and educational institutions.

While firms may take the lead in organizing and developing training programs, substantial governmental participation will be necessary if such programs are to be established on an adequate scale. The economic incentives for firms displacing workers, for unions, and for educational institutions are insufficient to ensure that an appropriate level of supply-push retraining programs will be implemented. This is because these groups are not the *principal* beneficiaries of retraining programs. Firms that displace workers may generate some publicity and good will from these programs and may be able to reduce other types of severance costs, but they generally have no need for the services of the retrained workers. Unions may improve the economic climate for their remaining members by helping displaced workers find new careers, but in the process they lose dues-paying members.

The main beneficiaries of these programs are the firms that will eventually hire retrained workers, the retrained workers themselves, and the general public (which is relieved of the responsibility of paying unemployment insurance benefits and welfare payments). The firms that will hire retrained workers, however, generally cannot be identified beforehand and, in fact, may not yet even be in existence. The workers who receive retraining are frequently incapable of financing their own retraining. As a result, the burden of undertaking these programs, if they are to be successful, falls largely on the government. We will examine several recent examples of government initiatives and other forms of community response in the next section.

BACKGROUND ON PUBLIC TRAINING POLICIES

Prior to 1962 the government's retraining programs were restricted to demand-pull retraining of its own employees. As a major employer it undertook training responsibilities both with respect to the military and its civilian workforce. In 1961 the federal government did undertake a limited ($13 million) program to train nongovernment employees under the Area Redevelopment Act,[60] but the 1962 Manpower Development and Training Act (MDTA) was the first major government program for nongovernment workers. This was at the time of the "automation crisis" of the 1960s. The national unemployment rate had reached 7 percent and there was a growing fear that technological and economic changes were rapidly displacing adult mid-career workers.[61] Hence the initial focus of the original MDTA program was to retrain unemployed adults, especially those who were unemployed as a result of technological change.

Training under MDTA could either take the form of institutional training in vocational education facilities or on-the-job training, though as a practical matter, very little of the funding was used for on-the-job training.[61] Both the costs of training and some living allowances were covered by the program. Most training of individuals lasted about 4 to 5 months.

While the original intention of the legislation was to train workers displaced by automation, by 1963 it was sufficiently clear that the automation scare had been premature at least, and perhaps nonexistent. During this period, however, the nation also had become aware of a significant population of poorly educated, low-skilled workers with unstable employment histories. Thus in 1963, MDTA was amended to redirect the program toward training minority youth and the disadvantaged. Under the revised program, up to one-quarter of the funds could be spent on training allowances for individuals under age 22, and funding was also made available for literacy training.[61]

MDTA was the only major federal government program designed to retrain workers displaced by technology. Several programs that included retraining components followed MDTA; these included the Neighborhood Youth Corps, the Work Experience and Training Program, the Job Corps, and the Comprehensive Employment and Training Act (CETA). All of these programs, however, were basically antipoverty programs geared toward offering training or work experience to disadvantaged youths or adults.

More recently the Trade Adjustment Assistance Program (part of the Trade Act of 1974) was designed to provide compensation and training for workers who were displaced by foreign competition. Under this program, groups of workers may petition the Department of Labor's Office of Trade Adjustment Assistance for benefits if they can demonstrate that employment and sales of their previous employer have declined, that imports of directly competitive products have increased, and that customers of the firm were substituting imported goods for domestic goods. The program applies only to directly displaced workers. Thus, while U.S. auto workers were able to qualify, employees of hard-hit suppliers to the automotive industry were not eligible.[62]

Between 1975 and 1980 over a million individuals had received benefits totaling $2.4 billion from the Trade Adjustment Assistance Program. The program is heavily tilted toward compensation rather than training, however. During this period more than 350,000 people had applied for employability services but less than 8 percent of these actually entered training, and fewer than 13,000 completed training.[63] The two largest groups served by this program were auto workers and steelworkers. A U.S. General Accounting Office study found that paperwork delays in the program resulted in most individuals receiving their benefits after they had returned to work.

In October 1982 a bipartisan consensus in Congress produced the Job Training Partnership Act (JTPA). The JTPA contains several significant departures from the earlier CETA program. In the first instance the JTPA provides a significantly increased role for state and local authorities. Under JTPA the federal government defines the overall objectives of the program, but the state governments have the basic managerial and coordinating functions. Design and implementation of the specific programs is left to local authorities.

A second significant departure of the JPTA is that the role of the business community is greatly expanded.[64] The law provides for the establishment of Private Industry Councils (PICs) that assist in the design of local training and placement programs. In addition, the PICs are to be involved in identifying local job opportunities for displaced workers and in identifying dislocated workers in the community.

Programs can be targeted to meet a variety of local needs such as major plant closings, counseling, job search, transportation, social services, pre-layoff assistance, and other services. Persons receiving benefits must either (1) have been terminated or have received notice of termination from their current employer with little likelihood that they will be able to return to their previous industry or occupation, or (2) have been, or will be, terminated as the result of a plant closure, or (3) have been unemployed for a long period with little chance of being employed in a similar occupation near where they live, or (4) are older individuals who may have substantial barriers to employment because of age. It is too early to assess the success of this fairly recent piece of legislation.

In addition to federal efforts, a wide variety of retraining programs have sprouted in the United States which are operated by state and local governments, by unions, by private employers, and by combinations of these sponsors. Four of these, the California Economic Adjustment Team, the Ford - United Auto Workers Program, the Downriver Community Conference Economic Readjustment Program, and the Des Moines Task Force on Plant Closings and Job Retraining, are typical of the scope of experimental programs offered.

The California Economic Adjustment Team

The State of California has been actively involved in designing programs to serve displaced workers. For example, in contrast to many states, unemployed individuals may receive employment benefits while they are engaged in retraining programs. Furthermore, in 1978 California passed the nation's first work-sharing legislation, encouraging employers that are facing a business decline to choose workweek reductions rather than layoffs. The affected employees may receive partial unemployment benefits while working reduced hours. Such arrangements facilitate training programs.

In 1980, California established the California Economic Adjustment Team (CEAT) to provide re-employment services to displaced workers. This team, staffed by the directors of the state's leading economic development agencies and institutions, enables the pooling of community, company, and labor resources to develop displaced worker retraining programs.[65]

Typically, the team becomes aware of the need for services either through voluntary firm notifications of impending plant closures or through the monitoring activities of the Department of Business and Economic Development (DBED). The CEAT team makes an assessment of whether the magnitude of the plant closure or layoff will require a coordinated response. Such a response is generally triggered when 1000 workers are laid off or a significant proportion of the labor force is dislocated. A number of strategies may then be pursued. For example, the DEBD may examine alternatives to plant closure, including employee buy-out, or the location of another business to occupy the facility. A dislocated worker re-employment center is generally established to find alternative jobs. In addition, retraining programs may be established in conjunction with local education facilities.[66] Whenever possible, the re-employment centers are located near or on the premises of the affected plant. The CEAT programs have ranged in length from 3 months to several years, but a typical program lasts for about 6 months.

The Ford - United Auto Workers Program

In its 1982 contract negotiations, Ford Motor Company and the United Auto Workers Union agreed to establish a joint training program for Ford's blue-collar employees. The program is funded by a 5-cent contribution on every dollar earned by Ford manufacturing employees. The program is jointly administered by Ford and the UAW through a governing body that provides overall policy guidance and authorizes program expenditures. The national program headquarters distributes funds to local UAW committees, performs technical evaluations of training programs, and provides other management and coordinating services to local committees. Actual retraining is decentralized, with local committees having the major responsibility for instituting and managing the programs. Training programs may be of several types. They may provide targeted vocational training for specific technical skills, placement services to help workers find new jobs outside the auto industry, tuition assistance, career counseling, and in-plant training.

Initially, the major focus of activities has been on retraining workers affected by plant closings or layoffs. Examples of current programs include a numerical control machine operator program in Alabama, a video production program in Tennessee, and a program dealing with the allied health professions in Michigan. In addition to funding provided in the Ford - UAW contract, additional money for these programs has been obtained from the U.S. Department of Labor, from state departments of labor education and employment security, and from federal trade assistance funds.

The Downriver Community Conference Economic Readjustment Program

The Downriver Community Conference (DCC) was one of the prime contractors under the CETA program. Since 1980, the DCC has operated a program to retrain workers in Wayne County, Michigan. While a main thrust of the program is to help displaced workers through job search assistance and retraining, another portion of the program is specifically geared toward employers.[67] Particularly for small businesses operating at or below 75 percent of capacity, the program assists in the expansion into new markets, largely by helping with the paperwork necessary to win defense contracts.

The retraining aspect of this program is operated through formal courses, generally conducted at local community colleges. Courses involve 28 to 36 hours of classroom instruction per week for between 8 and 39 weeks depending on the course. Recent courses have included cable television installation and maintenance, auto body repair, computer occupations, numerical control, and pipe welding.

Des Moines Task Force on Plant Closings and Job Retraining

In response to the announced plans of two major employers to shut down manufacturing facilities in the Des Moines, Iowa area, a task force was established to aid displaced workers.[68] Massey-Ferguson, Inc., a machine parts producer, and Wilson Foods, Inc., a food packaging firm, laid off approximately 1200 workers. In addition, local studies showed that an additional 3000 workers were likely to be laid off as a result of other impending plant closings.

The task force established two transition centers for employee counseling, skills assessment, and referral services. Training was provided by a number of local educational facilities, including a private university, local community colleges, and the public school system. Funding for this program was received from a variety of sources, including CETA, the Governor's Office, the U.S. Department of Labor, and the Massey-Ferguson Company. The job placement rate for those completing the job search assistance program was about 65 percent.

Clearly, the beginnings of some retraining efforts for technologically displaced workers are underway in the United States, though these efforts are generally small-scale and have met with mixed success. To find examples of larger-scale programs coordinated on a national level, it is necessary to look at the experience of other countries. Because the Swedish retraining program is relatively mature and has served as the model for many other countries, it is useful to focus briefly on its design.

RETRAINING IN SWEDEN

The public sector provision of retraining for unemployed workers in Sweden is part of a comprehensive package of labor market policies that also includes the employment service (vacancy information, job counseling, and placement assistance), financial assistance (training and relocation allowances, unemployment benefits, and wage subsidies), and job creation (public sector employment, and regional and sectoral employment stimulus programs). All of these programs are administered by a single agency, the Labor Market Administration (LMA) which is attached to the Ministry of Labor. The LMA has an extensive field organization for the implementation of its operations, with governing boards at the national, county, and district levels that consist of representatives of union and employer organizations, local officials, and LMA administrators. The participation of union and employer representatives in policy formulation and implementation (though not detailed management) is viewed as being an important element in gearing labor market policy to varying conditions in local labor markets.

Training administered by the LMA is provided in several contexts, both within firms and outside firms, and the relative importance of various training mechanisms have varied over time. In-plant training accounted for 6 percent of all participants in 1982, down from a peak of 35 percent in 1977, when it played an important role in cushioning the impact of steel and shipbuilding industry crises.

Most of the training that occurs outside of plants occurs in LMA-sponsored training programs in Labor Market Training Centers. While the curricula offered in these centers are essentially the same as that in secondary- or junior-college-level vocational education programs, the courses are intentionally conducted in a manner that resembles the workplace rather than the classroom, led by teachers who have had at least 7 years of industrial experience. This is done to maximize the applicability of training to potential jobs.

The courses provided at the centers emphasize training in generic skills that are applicable to jobs beyond those that will be obtained immediately after the completion of training. Remedial education is offered where necessary as a prerequisite for occupational training. This tends to be limited, however, and is tied as closely as possible to the anticipated occupational training.

The occupations for which training is provided are selected by the LMA on the basis of its information about available vacancies. This information is more readily available in Sweden (and other Western European countries) than in the United States, because, as noted above, employers are legally obligated to report vacancies to the national employment service and private employment agencies are prohibited by law. The information the LMA receives through the employment service and through more informal contacts with local labor market experts includes more than existing vacancies. The LMA also acquires information on likely future vacancies that may be anticipated as a result of known plans, observed developments, and expected trends. Swedish officials, however, believe that it is impossible to try to determine the needed volume and composition of course offerings over extended periods on the basis of long-term labor market forecasts. Instead, emphasis is placed on maintaining program flexibility to adapt quickly to changing circumstances. The relevant planning horizon is about 1 year.

Retraining in Sweden is closely linked to placement. To be eligible for retraining, applicants must have sought help from the employment service, and the employment service must judge that training is necessary for a person to secure a steady job. Placement officers, located in training centers, work with trainees to help them find jobs before the retraining courses are completed.

Training allowances for income maintenance are provided to participants in LMA courses at the same level as would be provided by the otherwise available unemployment insurance benefits. The top benefit rate is almost equal to the average wage in Sweden. In addition, employers can obtain wage subsidies and reimbursement for the costs of certain kinds of internal retraining programs.[69]

DESIGNING RETRAINING PROGRAMS FOR THE UNITED STATES

Although experience with retraining programs, particularly in a United States cultural context, is limited, there are some clear lessons to be derived concerning the appropriate design of worker retraining programs.

First, all of the parties whose support will be needed to make retraining successful should be directly involved in designing and implementing retraining programs. Effective retraining programs will require the cooperation and enthusiastic support of workers, employers, unions, educators, and a variety of levels of government.

Foreign experience has shown that involvement at the national level is important if retraining policies are to be linked to other labor market and macroeconomic policies. In particular, linkage to a nationwide system geared toward determining the appropriate skills to be included in retraining programs and a regional (if not nationwide) job vacancy identification and placement service is critical for ensuring that workers are retrained for jobs that will, in fact, exist.

Other factors dictate federal government involvement as

well. The tax base in local areas experiencing substantial worker displacement is unlikely to support retraining and job search programs of an appropriate magnitude. In addition, the benefits of these programs flow beyond the local area as workers relocate in areas where jobs are more plentiful. Consequently, it seems advisable that a significant fraction of the funding for such programs should be generated from broader-based funding sources.

While federal funding participation is important, state and local participation will ensure that the specific programs are designed to meet local needs and that they will operate successfully in the local cultural environment. Unlike many European nations, the United States is a heterogeneous society with widely differing needs that demand a range of different programs.

Surveys of future job opportunities on an occupation by occupation basis are speculative at best. For this reason, the occupational targets of retraining programs should be kept flexible, so changes can be made continuously and with relatively brief time lags. Sweden seems to have been particularly successful in this area by tying labor market information systems directly to the displaced worker program and maintaining relatively short planning horizons. Some localities in the United States have attempted to accomplish this objective by designing programs to meet a specific plant closing and terminating the program when the population of the plant has been serviced.

With regard to program design, the very limited experience in the United States makes it difficult to draw definitive conclusions. It does seem clear, however, that training should begin as soon as possible after layoffs occur. This will minimize the impact on the displaced worker's morale and pocketbook and ensure that he or she is reintegrated into the labor force as soon as possible. Furthermore, placement and training facilities should be located as close to the worker's old job location as is feasible. The retraining program should be designed to mirror the work environment (rather than a school environment). Instructors should have substantial industrial experience in addition to teaching experience. Finally, retraining programs should capitalize on those assets and facilities that are already available. Counseling should be provided so individuals can be placed in training programs that build on skills they already possess, and existing education and training delivery systems should be recruited and adapted to the needs of displaced workers.

12

PLANT LOCATION, ORGANIZATION, RELATIONSHIPS, AND ATTITUDES

I t should be obvious to the reader by now that the impact of computer-integrated manufacturing processes will reach far beyond the factory floor. The changes will be different in nature as well as in scope. Incremental automation of the past 60 years or so has tended to have only modest consequences for people not directly connected with production operations. The same has been true thus far for the few large firms who have invested in one or two computer-integrated systems. The amount of production converted to the new systems has been too small to have a wider effect. Once computer-based systems become pervasive, however, the effects will be felt throughout the company. Until very recently, the continuous-process industries have provided the only concrete illustrations of the potential extent of the transformation that can be expected. Experience in these industries indicates that change will reverberate throughout the manufacturing company, producing restructured organizations, altered relationships, new perspectives about time, and new competitive strategies. With change come opportunities for radically improved performance.

The major portion of this book has been devoted to the immediate effects of computer/telecommunications technology on people in the workforce. We have focused primarily on displacement, job content, and skills needs. These were the areas most emphasized by the executives we interviewed. In this final chapter, we consider options for dealing with some of the other people-related issues that will be of major importance to managements of companies in the years ahead:

☐ *Plant location* is a continuing issue for companies contemplating major automation installations, and it is of major concern to the communities in which plants are presently situated.

☐ Changes in *organizational structure* of companies are usually considered to be of concern only to managers and professionals; computer/telecommunications technologies will produce organizational changes affecting production workers, as well.

☐ *Relationships* among people in a firm will change. There will be controversy over "turf" and status, loss of customary affiliations, and changes in formal and informal groupings and degree of social interaction. The traditional management/worker interface will be irrelevant in a workforce where every individual shares responsibility in a production team.

☐ Each of the changes implicit in the introduction of computer/telecommunications technology will have some effect on the *attitudes* of individuals in the workforce, and people's attitudes will determine whether automation attempts succeed.

In each of these aspects of technology impact there are opportunities for great benefits for the firm that manages change well. The gains will come through careful planning and skillful implementation. If the technology chosen is appropriate for the production task, and if human factors are recognized and designed into the change, a firm should be in position to capitalize on new dimensions of competitive strength.

NEW PLANT/OLD PLANT; NEW LOCATION/OLD LOCATION

There are two basic issues relative to the site of new manufacturing technology. One is the question of continued location in the present community versus relocation. The second question is relevant only to the firm that elects to remain in the same location: whether to renovate an existing plant facility or to acquire a new plant.

Remaining in the same community has a number of advantages. The firm is able to retain valuable, trained employees and to maintain their loyalty to the firm. By keeping existing community ties, the firm continues to use an established infrastructure of suppliers and services. At a time when primary attention must be devoted to the installation of the new manufacturing system and the reorientation of the workforce in this system, adjustments to a new community add to the complexity of the task.

There are arguments for putting new systems into existing plants. All aspects of a plant currently in use are known, both the good points and the bad. There should be fewer surprises. Frequently, an old plant has a much greater real value than is shown on the company books, because it has been fully depreciated or because its acquisition cost was low. Real estate and other property taxes on an older plant may be lower than for a new plant. Plant occupancy costs, consequently, can be kept low. The automated system may be able to tie into existing systems of materials inventory, shipping and receiving, maintenance, assembly or other nonautomated parts of the production process. Replication of these activities is avoided. From a human resource standpoint, placing the new system in an existing, operating plant makes it possible for employees to participate in the transition, to get a feel for the new processes, and even to assist in decisions relating to them.

There are also negative aspects of staying in the same plant. If you are trying to maintain production output at the same time you are undergoing major renovation, the changeover can be difficult. One firm that attempted it had to subcontract a large fraction of its production work for almost a year while the plant was renovated and the new equipment was put in place and debugged. During this time roughly 2500 of the 3000 employees in the plant were either transferred to other company plants in the area or laid off. The manufacturing organization in that plant had to be rebuilt almost from scratch once the machines were ready to run. If they had installed the new systems in a new building, it would have been possible for the older system to continue producing until phased out by the new system.

A new plant also allows manufacturing engineers to design the system and place machines without having to compromise with existing plant configurations. In a new plant it may be possible to incorporate efficiencies that reduce building operating costs, that facilitate materials movement and storage, or that provide more attractive working surroundings.

The decision to relocate a plant to another community or state tends to be made on nontechnological grounds. A major consideration in such moves is the possiblity of a more favorable economic climate. Wage levels may be lower, necessary labor skills may be more plentiful, taxes and utilities costs may be lower, and unions may be absent. For many firms, the move to a new location permits a thoroughgoing housecleaning, getting rid of "deadwood" among employees, and eliminating costly, constraining work rules and practices.

Relocation may also be a means of splitting off part of an operation that has grown to unwieldy size. The result is a streamlined organization and a lower company profile in that community. Because communities have become increasingly sensitive to the issues of factory closures, a piecemeal shift may be a less threatening move than a full-scale shutdown and relocation.

State and local governments are becoming concerned about the social impacts of plant relocations. Legislation has been proposed in several states that would require a notification period before plants would be allowed to close. It is felt that

firms generate substantial costs for state and local governments when they decide to close plants. These costs cannot be
levied against a firm after it has left the area. Plant closing
legislation enacted at the local or state level, however, may
only generate more problems for the area affected: One of its
principal effects will be to discourage companies from locating
in areas that have such rules. It seems reasonable that the
costs a community must bear as a result of a plant closing
should be incorporated into the plant relocation decision.
This problem deserves to be studied at the federal level to see
if it is possible to formulate a national policy on plant relocations.

ORGANIZATIONAL STRUCTURE

A good many books have been written on the subject of the
organizational structure of industrial firms, and it is likely that
the forthcoming changes in technology will produce still more.
Instead of attempting a detailed appraisal of the organizational
options made possible by computer/telecommunications technology, we have concentrated on identifying those factors
that will make the new industrial environment different and,
therefore, will influence future organizational decisions.
These are some of the factors that future writers of organizational treatises are likely to contend with.

   We have repeatedly emphasized the need for swift human
response to problems originating in computer-integrated
manufacturing systems. Fast decisions are needed to avoid
prolonged, costly shutdowns of equipment or the manufacture of flawed products. A tightly coupled, high capital cost
system cannot tolerate slow, convoluted decision processes
that wind their way through various support organizations.
We have heard much about "just-in-time" inventory manage-

ment practices popularized by the Japanese. Computer-based systems will need just-in-time management responses.

Just-in-time management will be made possible by computer integration and analysis of information on a continuing basis. Managers can be brought up-to-date in a few minutes by interrogating their computer terminals. They will avoid the time-consuming practice of delegating a search for information to a crew of assistants. Computer-based expert systems, teleconferencing, and local area information networks will aid the decision-making process.

Machine integration will be paralleled by organizational integration. The interdependencies between materials availability, product quality, delivery schedules, and utilization of human and machine resources are very strong. To obtain fast responses, single individuals or integrated teams will be asked to make the decisions. The need for the professional specialist at the operating level is likely to become a thing of the past.

It follows logically that responsibility for operating decisions will be moved to the lowest posible level in the organization. This lowest level will frequently be that of a machine operator or technician who has greater familiarity with the process and who is more consistently available to make the choices.

The number of people needed to manufacture a given volume of output will decrease. The value and complexity of the manufacturing process will increase. These shifts will give different meaning to the concepts of responsibility and authority. The importance of a position in the organization will no longer be measured in terms of numbers of people supervised. The unit of measure will be a bit more elusive. It may be expressed in terms of the value of investment supervised, or the number of decisions that must be made, or the value of output, or the level of complexity of the system being managed. Whatever becomes the new basis for measuring responsibility also becomes the basis for performance evaluation and for reward.

If the thrust of operating decision-making is downward, then upper levels of management are freed up for strategic planning and decision-making. Assistance from computer information systems will be available at these levels, making large information-gathering staffs less necessary. Consequently, we expect that there will be a thinning out of staff groups supporting corporate-level executives who have become computer/communications literate. These managers will be able to reach into the communications net for information, by-passing their staffs and line managers. The emphasis in corporate headquarters will be for more stategists and fewer "go-fers" or information handlers. This shift may cause some upset and uncertainty, especially if computer-proficient executives suddenly appear in senior slots.[70] If subordinates are not proficient in computer-based analysis or if they cannot control the flow of information on their performance or the performance of their organization to their superior, the trauma may be severe.

Because senior executives will have more ready access to information about the firm, about competition, and about the economy, and because they will have delegated operating decisions to lower levels, they will be able to focus more attention on these key activities:

☐ *Strategic planning,* including technological strategies for products and processes.

☐ *Organization and improvement* of systems of people, machines, and information.

☐ *Evaluation* of the performance of all functions of the system for the purpose of improvement.

☐ *Communication* of goals, plans, and achievements, to all levels of the firm.

☐ *Human development* to maximize the capabilities and contributions of all employees in the firm.

The organization of machines, of people, and of information now become three concomitant aspects of the design of a production system. Design of organizations is open to options made possible by technology. Firms are not locked into one conceptual scheme, but are free to create structures that fit with their mode of operation and corporate philosophy. Computer and telecommunications aids can be tailored to make a given organizational scheme work. In this respect, the design of organizations and the design of jobs have much in common. Neither subject should be taken up for the purpose of making changes without considering this linkage.

RELATIONSHIPS

We repeat: The quality of human relationships in firms employing advanced manufacturing technology will depend on how well the total system of people, machines, and information is designed. There are excellent prospects for significant improvements in the manufacturing milieu that will contribute to better human interactions, but there are also strong possibilities that relationships will suffer. It will not be the technology that makes the difference; it will be the way managers and designers use the technology.

What are the differences between a positive set of human relations in a firm and a set of relationships that have gone sour? Let us review the realities of computer-based automation from the viewpoint of the worker in the plant. There will be fewer people in a plant, so there will be the potential for greater isolation of individuals, each responsible for a segment of the system. Communications will frequently be remote, that is, by telephone, intercom, or computer terminal, rather than face-to-face. The nature of work will shift from physical activity to monitoring and mental activity. Many of the tasks previously done by people will now be done by machines and computers. The work will be safer and the work area may be cleaner, quieter, and more attractive. Workers will have less collective power. The cohesive force provided by strong unions in the past will no longer be a support to the worker.

It becomes evident that among these changes there are ample reasons for concern about future human relationships in computer-integrated manufacturing systems. Why, then, do we optimistically say there are excellent opportunities for improved relations?

There may be physical isolation, but there *can be* substantial interdependence and interaction. What one portion of the system does is likely to influence directly the performance of other parts of the system. Workers will be monitoring machines, rather than physically controlling them; this will enable workers to become more mobile, to help others in a crisis, consult with supervisors, trade-off jobs, and to act as participants in a team. A team spirit can be promoted by management through flexible or rotating work assignments, common training programs, group problem-solving sessions, and access to a communications network.

Where unions exist, the task of creating a positive human relations environment could be more difficult, largely because of the history of adversarial relations between management and labor. Unions, however, have shown a rather consistent pattern of acceptance of technological change in recent years. If weakened unions are met with managements that are willing to share information, to include workers in planning change, to design jobs for challenge and growth, to ease transitions of employees that are displaced, and to share the gains of increased productivity equitably, a new climate of worker/management cooperation and trust may emerge.

The cumulative effects of traditional antagonisms and past practices are likely to be the major causes for failures in human relationships in plants adopting computer-integrated systems. If managements perpetuate many of these largely unsuccessful strategies from the past, they will destroy all hope of achieving competitive strength through technological change. It would be relatively simple, because of the nature of the new technology, to design jobs that are truly isolated, jurisdictionally compartmentalized, reduced to elemental routines, and that promise no opportunity for growth or advancement. It would be possible for managements who are guided by past practices to structure the reward system of a firm so all the benefits of automation flow to managers and owners (and to the government). It would certainly be possible, by creating labor surpluses and by de-skilling jobs, to drive down the price paid for labor. Such steps, however, will only lead to resistance, lack of cooperation, delay, and, ultimately, irretrievable loss of the competitive edge that is being sought. Managements in a great many companies will have to be alert to the danger that, if they make no effort to replace old behavioral norms in the firm, these steps will be followed.

To illustrate how traditional thinking can lead to unconscious repetitions of past mistakes, we cite a conversation we had in one of the plants of a highly respected, progressive manufacturing firm. The subject was whether to design jobs to permit social interaction during work:

Manufacturing engineer:

"You have to realize that human beings . . . like to socialize, and if you take all that contact away from them, I agree you have a problem. But, there is the working environment and then there is something to take care of the person. That is still a problem . . . on how far you go on this one. We put in lunch centers and all this kind of business to try to bring a more human element into the shop. But once a person goes back to work, theoretically he goes back to *work*, and then he should not have this contact. But, he should be able to have the contact afterwards."

The Human Resources representative of the firm asked:

"You don't allow him socialization while at work?"
"No."
"You have not designed it into the work itself?"
"No. In (plant name) what we did was we designed the place where he has his recreation time lunching, with landscaping and trees and banks and things like that..."

Consultant:

"Do you know what you are doing? You are creating an environment where there is greater incentive to be *away* from the job than to be on it, to perform more competently *away* from the job than in it."

Human Resources representative:

"You might be right . . . Yes, I believe that. I believe that's one of the things that happens in the world of work. We try to exhort people to set aside so much that we lose sight of the key thing about people—they need human interaction. . . ."

Manufacturing engineer:

"What you are saying is if you make (the lunchroom) like hell and make the job really interesting and nice and pleasant, then the worker is liable to be a productive person."

Human Resources representative:

"What works in human productivity is for people to be excited about their *jobs*, not excited about the lunchroom. That's what we did, though."

ATTITUDES

Each of the issue areas involving management strategy that have been discussed in this book has some bearing on employee attitudes. These attitudes, in turn, play an important part in whether technological change proceeds smoothly and rapidly or whether it stumbles along in a fog of suspicion, fear, and controversy. Both the means used to solve the various issues and the processes of arriving at these solutions will influence attitudes.

During our investigation we have become aware of a number of possible negative feelings that may be encountered during the change to computer-based automation and advanced communications technology:

1. Personal doubts about ability to perform, because of skills or knowledge gaps.
2. Loss of sense of control over meaningful aspects of the job.
3. Distrust of the use that superiors might make of systems that carry far more information about employees' performance.
4. Loss of opportunity for personal growth and advancement.
5. Antagonism toward new job parameters.
6. Fear of displacement.

These concerns are universal; they are not confined to the blue-collar workforce. Each item is equally applicable to staff employees and to middle managers.

On the other hand, with conscious and sensitive planning, the adoption of these new technologies can be the source of very positive reactions:

1. Ability to use higher-level skills and intelligence on the job.

2. Increased sense of control and involvement in a broader job.

3. Higher individual visibility and recognition in smaller organizations.

4. Opportunity to learn, grow, advance.

5. Relief in getting away from dangerous, harmful, or dehumanizing jobs.

6. Opportunity to see results of contributions to the economic health of the firm.

There is close correspondence between the positive viewpoints and the negative reactions. Some of the points are like bright and dark sides of the same coin. We reiterate: It is not the technology itself that will produce either favorable or unfavorable responses; it is the strategy behind the changes that makes the difference. It is the strategy employed by managers and technologists within a firm, and it is the policies that guide public agencies such as schools, training centers, employment offices, and the like, that determine how people feel about their jobs, their employers, and their future.

Those who experience the negative impacts of technological change may come to regard *technology* as the enemy. They should not. Their problems are caused by human decisions, made in the context of corporate and public policies, that dictate how technology is to be applied and how people are to be treated. Their quarrel should be with those who, consciously or by default, fail to foresee the consequences of technological change. Their quarrel should be with those who fail to redefine the nature of jobs, of roles, and of organizational relationships in the light of impending change. Instead of blaming technology, employees should expect that managers at every level will work with technologists to ensure that technology is used creatively and constructively to further human capabilities. They should expect that institutions and agencies of the community will provide them with relevant work skills, job information, and assistance, so they can adapt flexibly to changes in the nature of work and employment.

If (as we maintain) policies and practices of people responsible for applying new technology can make the difference between acceptance and opposition to change, then managers who set policies might be able to use some guidelines within which to shape policy. Let us sum up the various points we have made about strategic responses to computer/ telecommunications technology and its impacts by highlighting a few basic precepts that underlie what we have recommended. Adoption of these ideas could be a first step toward a new climate for manufacturing.

The first of these precepts is that managers must realize how important it is that every employee has a sense of personal security. Personal security is a concept that goes beyond job security. Personal security means that even a person being displaced or being laid off must perceive his or her situation as one in which there are provisions for job location or relocation, training, some degree of income maintenance, and a preservation of earned rights and benefits.

In the American industrial environment it is unrealistic to presume that many firms will provide the measure of personal security afforded by guarantees of lifelong employment. The task, therefore, of creating an environment of general personal security must be shared by major sectors of our society. The pre-eminent role belongs to industry, but local, state, and national agencies of government must be involved. Because technological changes are evolutionary, long-term phenomena, the role of government must be dependable and predictable, not crisis-driven. There must be effective interaction between industry and government agencies at all levels, to facilitate employment and match worker skills to available jobs. Educational institutions, public and private, help to create personal security when they give the student a chance to develop job competencies and when they give students accurate guidance on career choices. We have suggested that other public services are needed to bolster personal security: a national job placement service, retraining programs, and relocation assistance.

A second precept is that employees at all levels of a firm must be allowed to share the benefits of technological change. If the "What's in it for me?" question has a positive answer for large numbers of people in the American workforce, it will be difficult to stifle the spirit of acceptance and cooperation essential to economic growth. Various firms will find different ways to satisfy the principle of sharing. The most difficult part will be to figure out how to compensate those most adversely affected—the employees who are laid off.

These first two principles, job security and sharing of benefits, are analogous to what Frederick Herzberg calls "hygiene" factors in the work environment.[71] The presence of these factors does not necessarily motivate a workforce to peak performance, but if they are absent, it is impossible to achieve any level of motivation. As Abraham Maslow would put it, these are lower-level needs that must be satisfied before human beings can go on to higher levels of attainment.[72]

The next principles address the question of motivation: What must be in a job to encourage a person to work at his or her highest level of capability? First, we must exploit the extraordinary flexibility of computer/telecommunications technology to design systems of people, machines, and information where the capabilities of both people and machines are maximized. To accomplish this requires managements to set policies for design and selection of technology that recognize human needs and attributes. Corporate policy should require managers and engineers to pay attention to the principles of good job design *before* the system hardware design is irrevocably frozen. Often the decision to revamp a plant or to build a new one is made too late, putting extreme time pressure on those responsible for providing the systems. Their response is to bend every effort to get the hardware contracts awarded as quickly as possible and to avoid consideration of the "soft" aspects of the change (human interfaces, skills levels, pay levels, information requirements) until much later. Frequently this haste at the start results in prolonged delays and disappointment at the other end.

Finally, there must be opportunity within the firm for individual participation, growth, and advancement concurrent with technological change. This principle relates partly to job design, but it looks beyond the design of individual production systems to the need for a corporate culture in which these values are considered essential to the well-being of the firm. Early involvement of all employees that will be affected by technological change has been advocated by both management and employee groups. Involvement means more than a vaguely worded notice in the company newsletter. It means dialogue: sharing in planning and implementation efforts. Such actions remove the mystery surrounding changes that will have been signaled by the grapevine. They serve to motivate employees to get ready for job transitions, and they free employees to take part in job design and design of the technology itself.

Most of these policies have one common requirement—they should be put into effect *before* major technological transitions occur. Changes in technology are easy, as compared to gaining or sustaining employee cooperation for those changes.

Computer/telecommunications technology will be adopted, slowly and inexorably, throughout industry. It will be much like the green revolution in agriculture in that respect. But that is where the similarity should end. If we know beforehand the nature of the technology, if we can shape its features to human needs and aspirations, and if we can avoid the pitfalls of applying traditional thinking to new opportunities, then we can act to employ this technological servant to our national advantage. This is an achievable goal worth pursuing.

REFERENCES

1. Juran, J. M., ed., *Quality Control Handbook*, 3rd edition. New York: McGraw-Hill, 1974.
2. Deming, W. Edwards, *Elementary Principles of Statistical Control of Quality*. Tokyo: Nippon Kagaku Gijutsu Renmei, 1950.
3. Crosby, Philip B., *Quality Is Free: The Art of Making Quality Certain*. New York: McGraw-Hill, 1979.
4. Hirschmann, Winfred B., "Profit from the Learning Curve," *Harvard Business Review*, January/February 1964.
5. Klein, Burton, *Dynamic Economics*. Cambridge, MA: Harvard University Press, 1977.
6. Skinner, Wickham, "Manufacturing: Missing Link in Corporate Strategy," *Harvard Business Review*, May/June 1969.
7. Hansen, John A., James I. Stein, and Thomas S. Moore, *Industrial Innovation in the United States*, report #84-1. Boston: Center for Technology and Policy at Boston University, August 1984.
8. For a more complete description of microprocessors and case examples of microprocessor applications in a variety of products, see Robert T. Lund, Marvin A. Sirbu, Jr., and James M. Utterback, *Microprocessor Applications: Cases and Observations*. London: Her Majesty's Stationery Office, 1980.
9. *Exploratory Workshop on the Social Impacts of Robotics: Summary and Issues*, Office of Technology Assessment. Washington: U.S. Government Printing Office, February 1982.
10. See also Carol Hymowitz, "Manufacturers Press Automating to Survive, but Results Are Mixed," *Wall Street Journal*, April 11, 1983, p. 1.
11. Hunt, H. Allan and Timothy L. Hunt, *Human Resource Implications of Robotics*. Kalamazoo, MI: W. E. Upjohn Institute for Employment Research, 1983.
12. Schonberger, Richard J., *Japanese Manufacturing Techniques*. New York: The Free Press, 1982.
13. Schmitt, Roland W., "Technological Trends," in *The Long-Term Impact of Technology on Employment and Unemployment*. National Academy of Engineering Symposium, June 30, 1983. Washington D.C.: National Academy Press, 1983.

14. Pollack, Andrew, "Lightwave Era Is Ushered In," *New York Times*, February 11, 1983.

15. "Business Bulletin," *Wall Street Journal*, March 31, 1983, p. 1.

16. Christensen, C. Paul, "Some Emerging Applications of Lasers," *Science*, Vol. 218, no. 4568, October 1982.

17. Abraham, Eitan, Colin T. Seaton, and S. Desmond Sineth, "The Optical Computer," *Scientific American*, Vol. 248, no. 2, February 1983.

18. Lindberg, R.A. and N.R. Braton, *Welding and Other Joining Processes*. Boston: Allyn and Bacon, 1976.

19. Abernathy, William J. and Utterback, James M., "Patterns of Industrial Innovation," *Technology Review*, June/July 1974.

20. Klein, Burton, "Productivity: A Dynamic Explanation," in *Technological Innovation for a Dynamic Economy*, Christopher T. Hill and James M. Utterback, eds. New York: Pergamon, 1979.

21. Abernathy, William J., Kim B. Clark, and Alan M. Kantrow, "The New Industrial Competition," *Harvard Business Review*, September/October 1981.

22. Reich, Robert B., *The Next American Frontier*. New York: Times Books, 1983.

23. National Academy of Engineering, Committee on Technology and International Economic and Trade Issues, Automobile Panel, *The Competitive Status of the U.S. Auto Industry: A Study of the Influences of Technology in Determining International Industrial Competitive Advantage*. Washington, D.C.: National Academy Press, 1982.

24. Hounshell, David A., *From the American System to Mass Production, 1800–1932*. Baltimore: Johns Hopkins University Press, 1984.

25. Birch, David L., *The Contribution of Small Enterprise to Growth and Employment*, M.I.T. Program on Neighborhood and Regional Change, M.I.T., Cambridge, MA, 1983.

26. Hayes, Robert H., "Why Japanese Factories Work," *Harvard Business Review*, July/August 1981.

27. Unpublished report describing effects of a major change to advanced automation technology in an industrial firm. Cambridge, MA: M.I.T. Center for Policy Alternatives, 1983.

28. Coffield, Theodore, "The Effects of Power Plant Automation on the Skill Level of the Workforce at Boston Edison," student research paper, M.I.T., May 1982.

29. Fadem, Joel, *Workforce Demographics and Their Implications for Human Resource Planning*. Los Angeles: Center for Quality of Working Life, Institute for Industrial Relations, UCLA, February 1982.

30. National Science Foundation, "Manufacturing Employment Becomes Increasingly Technological," *Science Resource Studies Highlights*, March 10, 1982.

31. Bureau of Labor Statistics, *Occupational Projections and Training Data*, 1980 Edition, Bulletin 2052, September 1980.

32. National Science Foundation, "Projected Unemployment Scenarios Show Possible Shortages in Some Engineering and Computer Specialties," *Science Resource Studies Highlights*, February 23, 1983.

33. Bureau of Labor Statistics, *Employment Trends in Computer Occupations*, Bulletin 2101, October 1981.

34. National Science Foundation, "Project Unemployment Scenarios Show Possible Shortages in Some Engineering and Computer Specialties," *Science Resource Studies Highlights*, February 23, 1983.

35. Hollomon, J. Herbert and Alan E. Harger, "America's Technological Dilemma," *Technology Review*, July/August 1971.

36. Smith, Adam, *An Inquiry into the Nature and Causes of the Wealth of Nations*. Modern Library Edition. New York: Random House, 1937.

37. Taylor, Frederick W., *The Principles of Scientific Management*. New York: Harper & Row, 1911.

38. Raskin, A. H., "The Negotiation," *New Yorker*, January 22 and 29, 1979.

39. Shaiken, Harley, *Work Transformed: Automation and Labor in the Computer Age*. New York: Holt, Rinehart & Winston, 1985.

40. Hayes, Robert H. and David A. Garvin, "Managing as if Tomorrow Mattered," *Harvard Business Review*, May/June 1982.

41. "The Interface Challenge. Report of the Committee on the CAD/CAM Interface, National Research Council," *American Machinist*, January 1985, p. 101.

42. Davis, Louis E., Ralph R. Canter, and John Hoffman, "Current Job Design Criteria," in *Design of Jobs*, Louis E. Davis and James C. Taylor, eds. Middlesex, England: Penguin Books, 1972.

43. Davis, Louis E., "The Design of Jobs," in *Design of Jobs*, Louis E. Davis and James C. Taylor, eds. Middlesex, England: Penguin Books, 1972.

44. Trist, Eric L., G. W. Higgin, H. Murray, and A. B. Pollack, *Organizational Choice*. Tavistock, England: Institute of Human Relations, 1963.

45. Skole, Robert, "Technology to Suit the Worker," *American Machinist*, September 2, 1974.

46. At Polaroid's Waltham, Massachusetts film-making plant, 1963.

47. At General Electric's Lynn, Massachusetts aircraft engine plant, 1968

to 1972. See Trudy Rubin, "Do Workers Work Better Without Bosses?" *Christian Science Monitor*, September 5, 1972.

48. At Digital Equipment Company's Enfield, Connecticut printed circuit board plant, 1984.

49. At Ingersoll-Rand's Roanoke, Virginia plant. See Nathan H. Cook, "Computer-Managed Parts Manufacture," *Scientific American*, February 1975.

50. Amrine, Harold T., John A. Ritchey, and Oliver S. Hulley, *Manufacturing Organization and Management*. Englewood Cliffs, NJ: Prentice-Hall, 1982.

51. Bylinsky, Gene, "America's Best-Managed Factories," *Fortune*, May 28, 1984.

52. Lincoln, James F., *Lincoln's Incentive System*. New York: McGraw-Hill, 1946.

53. Johannesson, Jan, *On the Composition of Swedish Labour Market Policy*, The Delegation for Labour Market Policy Research, Sweden, 1983.

54. Leve, Manfred, "Labor Market Policy in the Federal Republic of Germany." Paper prepared for Conference on European and American Labor Market Policies, Washington, D.C., 1981.

55. McCarthy, Maureen E. and Gail S. Rosenberg, *Work Sharing Case Studies*. Kalamazoo, MI: The W. E. Upjohn Institute, 1981.

56. Poor, Riva and James L. Steele, "Work and Leisure: The Reactions of People at 4-day Firms," in *4 Days, 40 Hours*, Riva Poor, ed. London: Pan Books, 1972.

57. Killingsworth, Charles C., "Cooperative Approaches to Problems of Technological Change," in *Adjusting to Technological Change*, G. S. Somers, E. L. Cushman, and N. Weinberg, eds. New York: Harper & Row, 1963.

58. "The Manufacturing Manager for the 1990's," a study being conducted by Robert T. Lund under National Science Foundation sponsorship, 1985.

59. National Academy of Engineering symposium, "Education for the Manufacturing World of the Future," Washington, D.C., September 20 -21, 1984.

60. Mangum, Garth, *The Emergence of Manpower Policy*. New York: Holt, Rinehart & Winston, 1969.

61. Advisory Committee on Intergovernmental Relations (ACIR), *The Federal Role in the Federal System: The Dynamics of Growth, Reducing Unemployment: Intergovernmental Dimensions of a National Problem*. Washington, D.C., February 1982.

62. Cprek, Kent G., "Worker Adjustment Assistance: Black Comedy in the Post-Renaissance," *Law and Policy in International Business*, Vol. 11, no. 2, pp. 593–690.

63. Johnston, Janet, "The National Employment and Training System," in National Commission for Employment Policy, *Seventh Annual Report: The Federal Interest in Employment and Training*, October 1981, pp. 61–103.

64. Gutman, Robert, "Job Training Partnership Act: New Help for the Unemployed," *Monthly Labor Review*, Vol. 106, no. 3, March 1983, pp. 3–11.

65. Fedrau, Ruth, "Strategies to Aid Workers Displaced by Plant Shutdowns and Mass Layoffs," Comments Prepared for the Workshop on Programs for Displaced Workers, National Association of Counties, July 12, 1982.

66. National Alliance of Business, "Bulletin: California Economic Adjustment Team," March 1983.

67. National Alliance of Business, "Bulletin: Downriver Community Conference Economic Readjustment," March 1983.

68. National Alliance of Business, "Bulletin: Mayor's Task Force on Plant Closings and Job Retraining," March 1983.

69. Hansen, John A., Andrew Martin, and James Maxwell, "Retraining Adult Workers for Jobs in the 1980s and 1990s: A Review of Past Programs, Current Proposals, and Future Needs." Prepared for the Office of Technology Assessment, U.S. Congress, October 1983.

70. See Mary Bralove, "Direct Data. Some Chief Executives Bypass and Irk Staffs in Getting Information," *Wall Street Journal*, January 12, 1983, p. 1.

71. Herzberg, Frederick, "One More Time: How Do You Motivate Employees?" *Harvard Business Review*, January/February 1968.

72. Maslow, Abraham H., *Motivation and Personality*. New York: Harper Bros., 1954.

INDEX